Scale 1: 500,000
or 8 miles to 1 inch
(5km to 1cm)

Reprinted June 2014
Reprinted October 2013
14th edition August 2013

© AA Media Limited 2014

GLOVEBOX ATLAS
BRITAIN

Cartography:
All cartography in this atlas edited, designed and
produced by the Mapping Services Department of
AA Publishing (A05243).

This atlas contains Ordnance Survey data
© Crown copyright and database right 2014
and Royal Mail data © Royal Mail copyright
and database right 2014.

Atlas contents

 This is based upon Crown
Copyright and is reproduced
with the permission of
Land & Property Services
under delegated authority from the Controller of
Her Majesty's Stationery Office, © Crown copyright
and database right 2014. PMLPA No. 100497.

 © Ordnance Survey Ireland/
Government of Ireland.
Copyright Permit No. MP0000314.

Map pages	II
Road map symbols	1
Road atlas Britain 1:500,000 scale	2–65
Index to places in Britain	66–81
County, administrative area map	66–67
Distance charts	68 & 90
Britain	68
Ireland	90
Road atlas Ireland 1:1 million scale	82–89
Index to places in Ireland	91–94

Publisher's notes:
Published by AA Publishing (a trading name of
AA Media Limited, whose registered office is
Fanum House, Basing View, Basingstoke,
Hampshire RG21 4EA, UK.
Registered number 06112600).

ISBN: 978 0 7495 7501 4 (paperback)

ISBN: 978 0 7495 7502 1 (wire bound)

A CIP Catalogue record for this book is available
from the British Library.

Disclaimer:
The contents of this atlas are believed to be correct
at the time of the latest revision, it will not contain
any subsequent amended, new or temporary
information including diversions and traffic control or
enforcement systems. The publishers cannot be
held responsible or liable for any loss or damage
occasioned to any person acting or refraining from
action as a result of any use or reliance on material
in this atlas, nor for any errors, omissions or
changes in such material. This does not affect your
statutory rights.

The publishers would welcome information to
correct any errors or omissions and to keep this
atlas up to date. Please write to the Atlas Editor,
AA Publishing, The Automobile Association, Fanum
House, Basing View, Basingstoke, Hampshire
RG21 4EA, UK.
E-mail: roadatlasfeedback@theaa.com

Printer:
Printed in Dubai by Oriental Press

GW00602805

Map pages

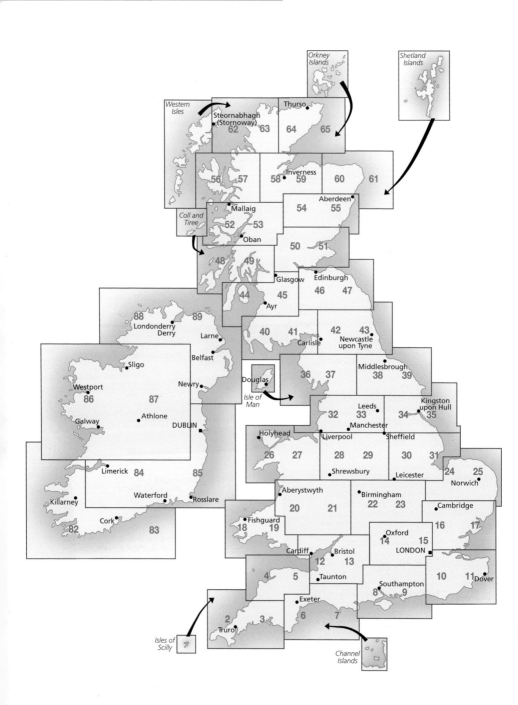

Road map symbols

Britain

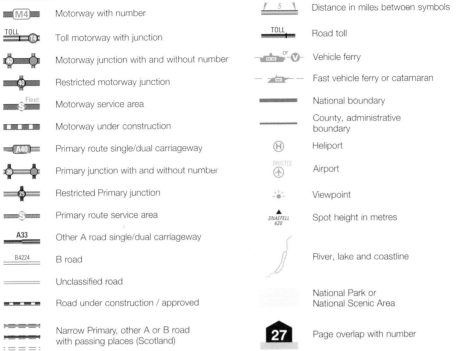

Motorway with number	Distance in miles between symbols
Toll motorway with junction	Road toll
Motorway junction with and without number	Vehicle ferry
Restricted motorway junction	Fast vehicle ferry or catamaran
Motorway service area	National boundary
Motorway under construction	County, administrative boundary
Primary route single/dual carriageway	Heliport
Primary junction with and without number	Airport
Restricted Primary junction	Viewpoint
Primary route service area	Spot height in metres
Other A road single/dual carriageway	
B road	River, lake and coastline
Unclassified road	
Road under construction / approved	National Park or National Scenic Area
Narrow Primary, other A or B road with passing places (Scotland)	Page overlap with number

1: 500 000   0   5   10 miles / 0 5 10 15 kilometres   8 miles to 1 inch

Ireland

Motorway	Primary route (Northern Ireland)
Toll motorway and booth	A road (Northern Ireland)
Motorway junctions with and without number	B road (Northern Ireland)
Restricted motorway junctions	Distance in miles between symbols (Northern Ireland)
Motorway service area	Minor Road
National primary route (Republic of Ireland)	Road under construction
National secondary route (Republic of Ireland)	International boundary
Regional road (Republic of Ireland)	Vehicle ferry
Distance in kilometres between symbols (Republic of Ireland)	Fast vehicle ferry or catamaran
Gaeltacht (Irish language area)	National Park

1: 1 000 000   0   10   20 miles / 0 10 20 30 kilometres   16 miles to 1 inch

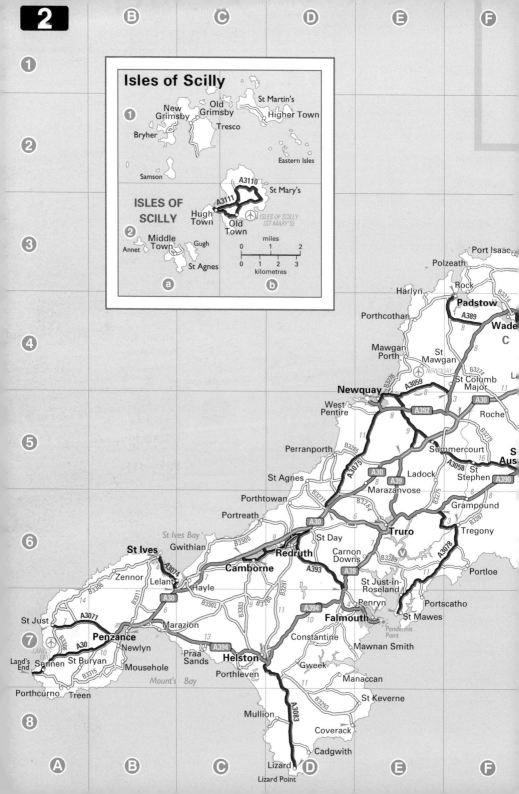

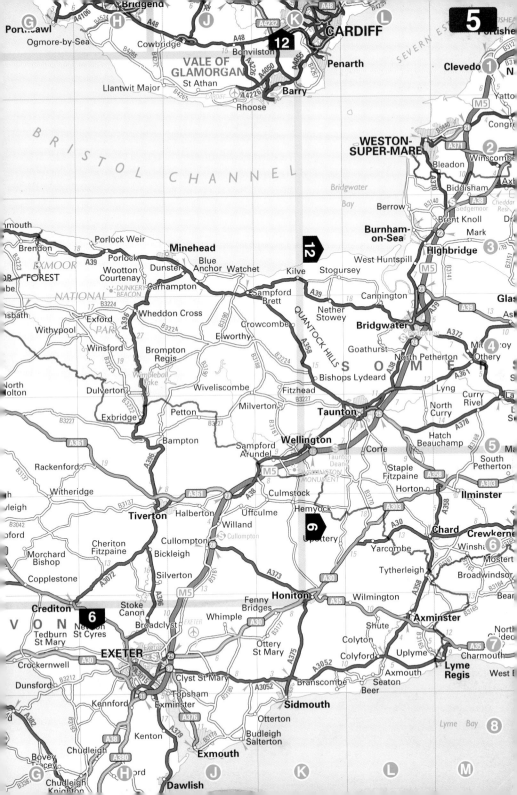

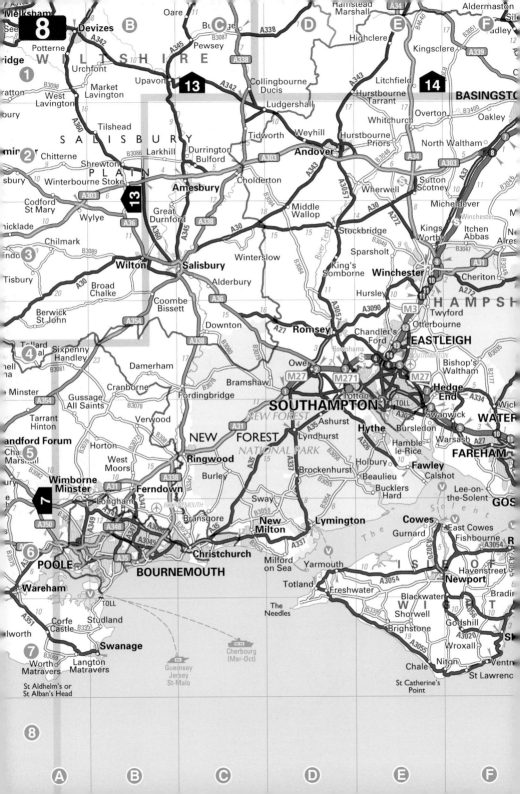

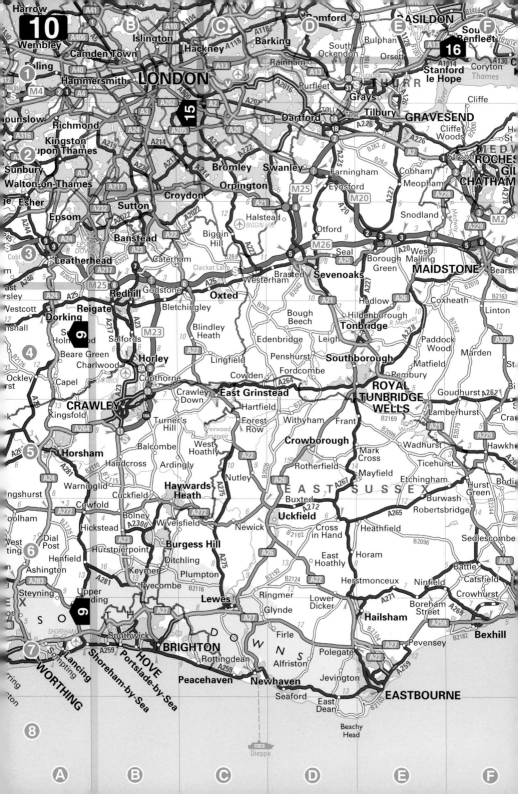

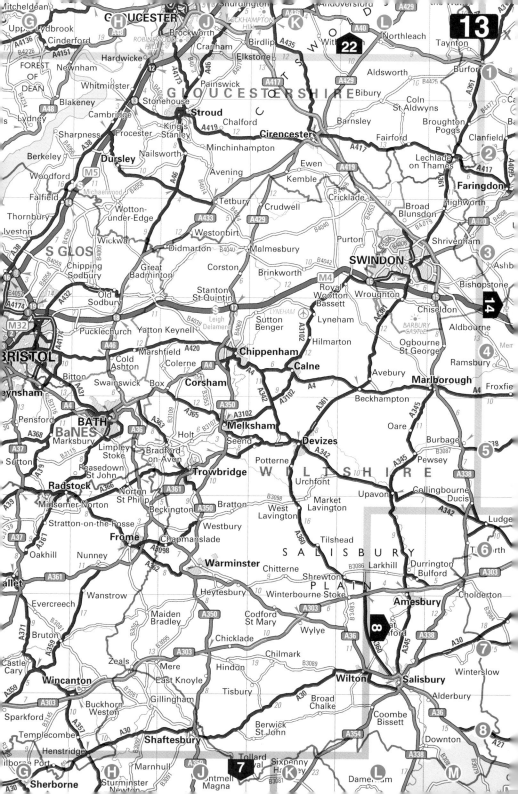

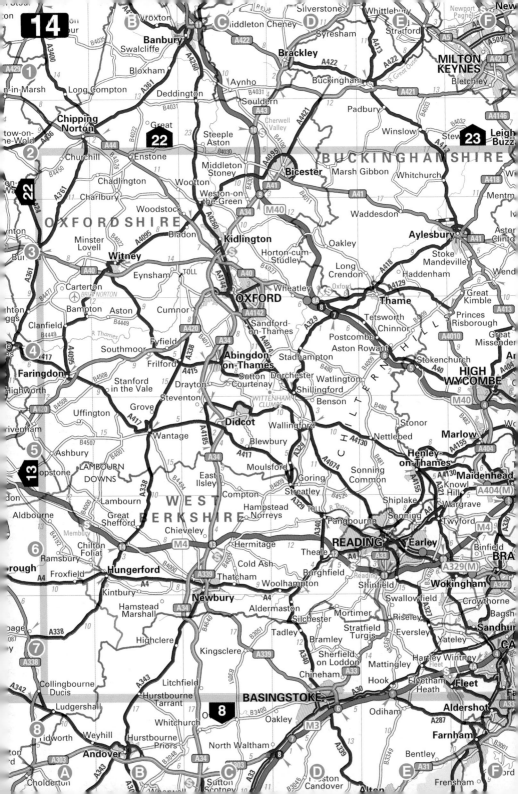

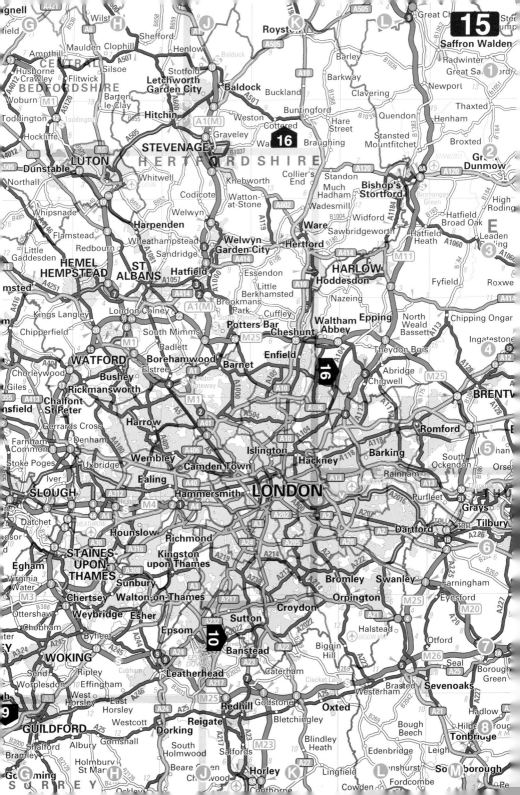

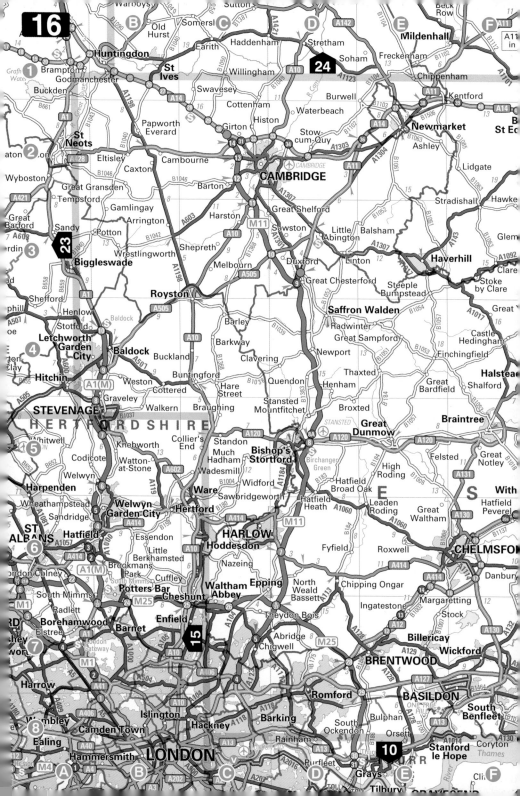

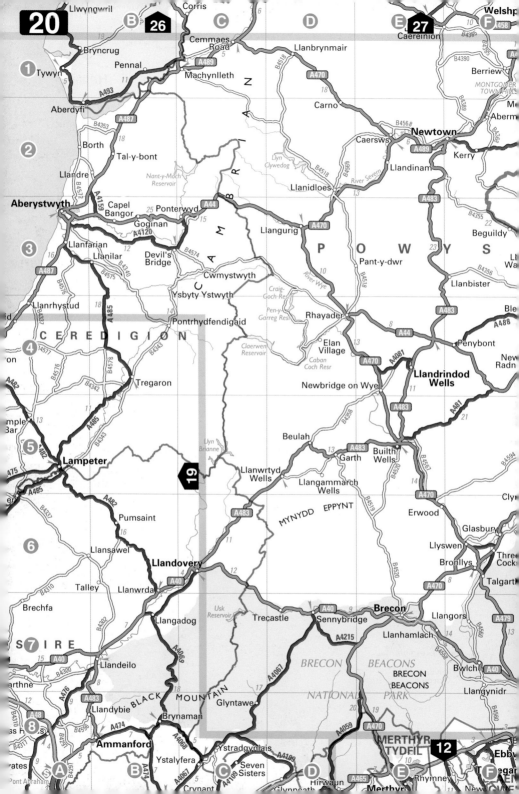

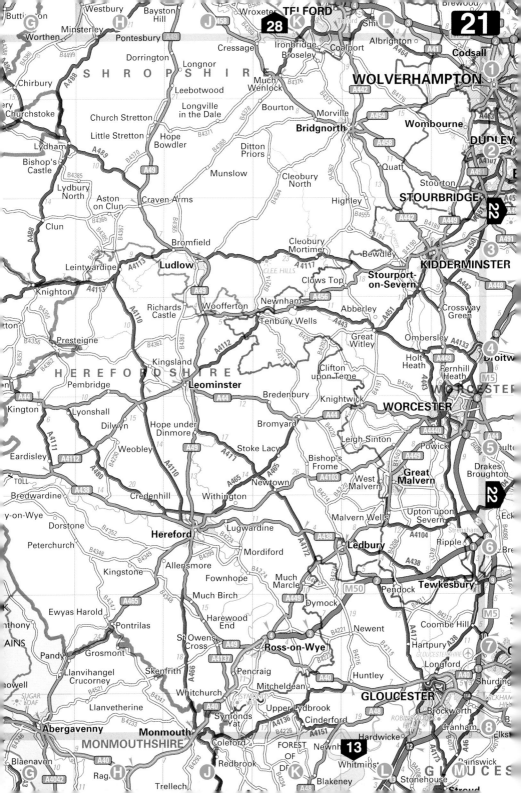

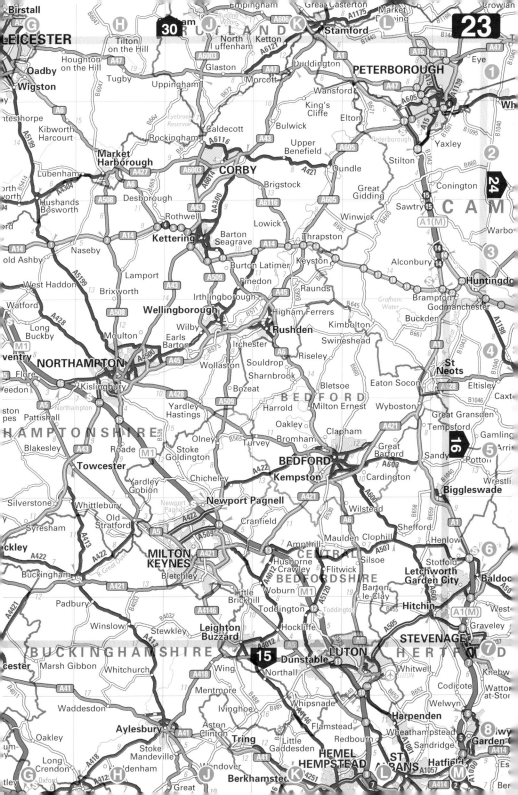

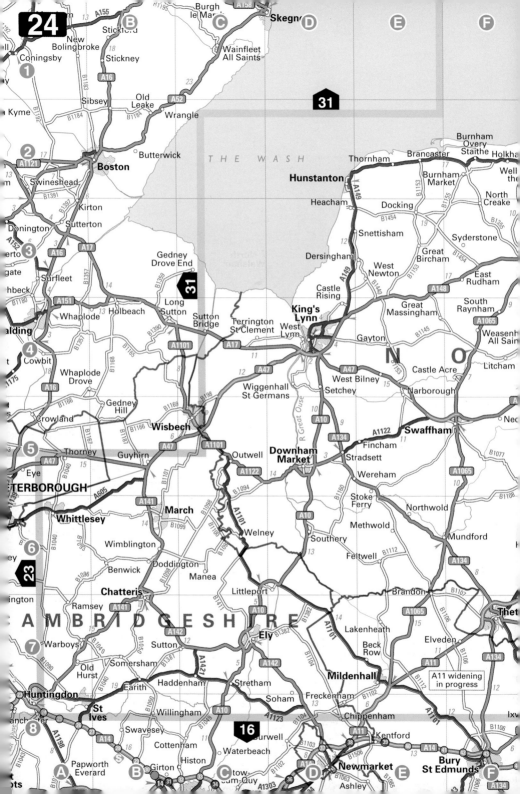

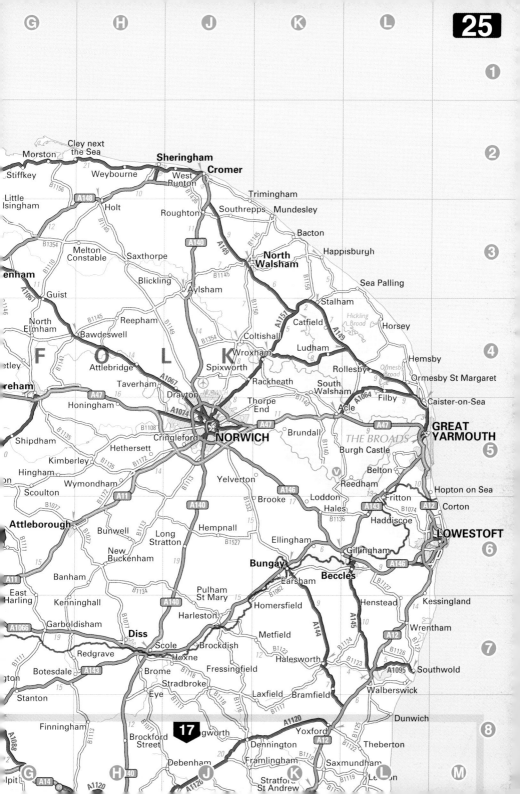

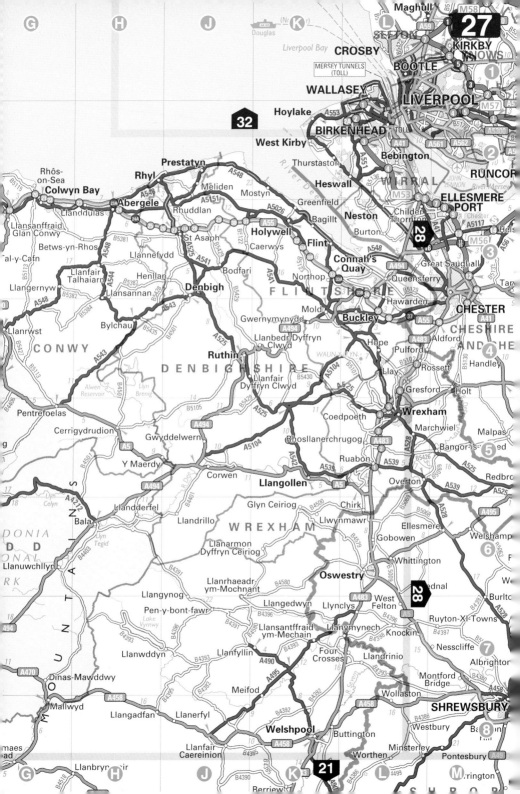

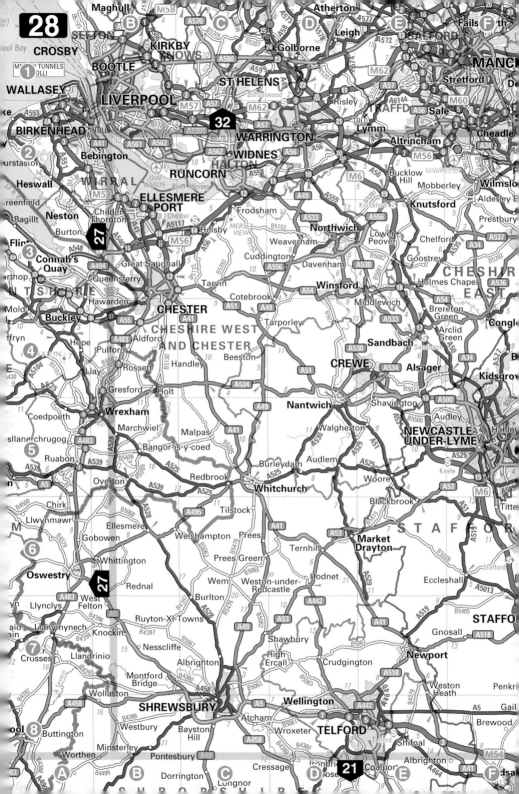

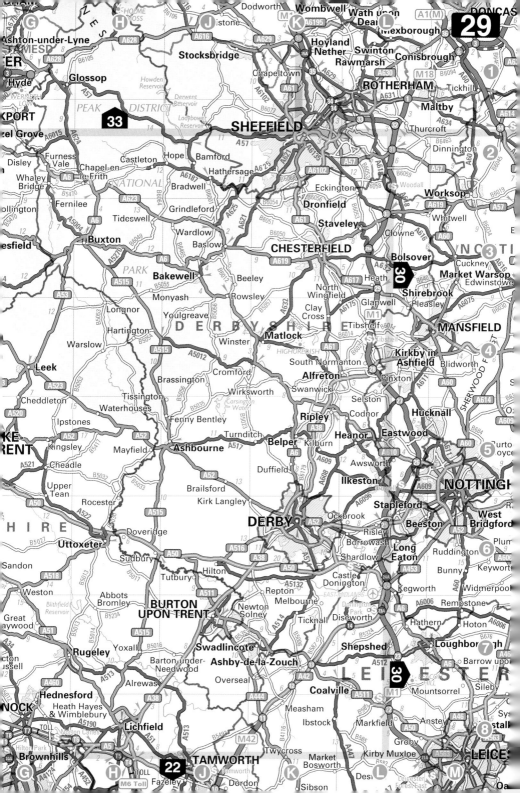

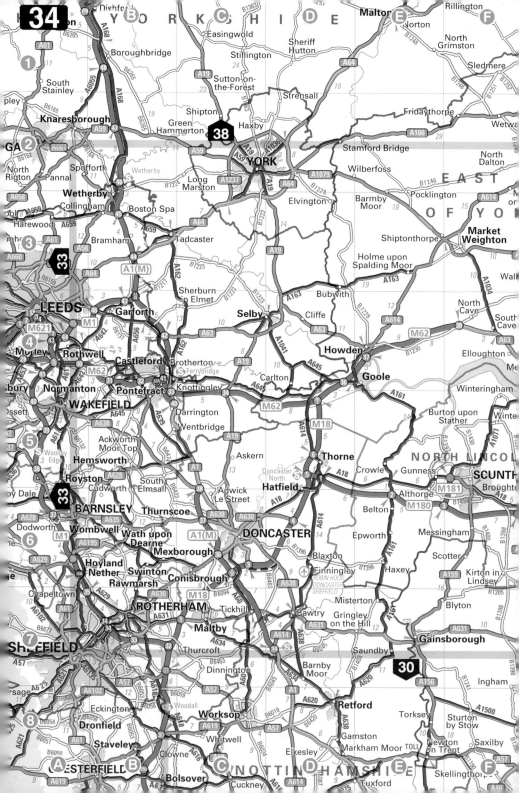

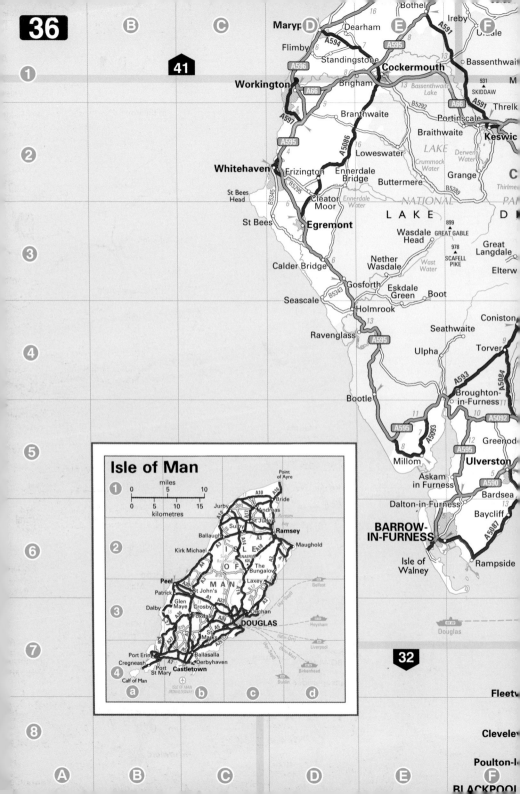

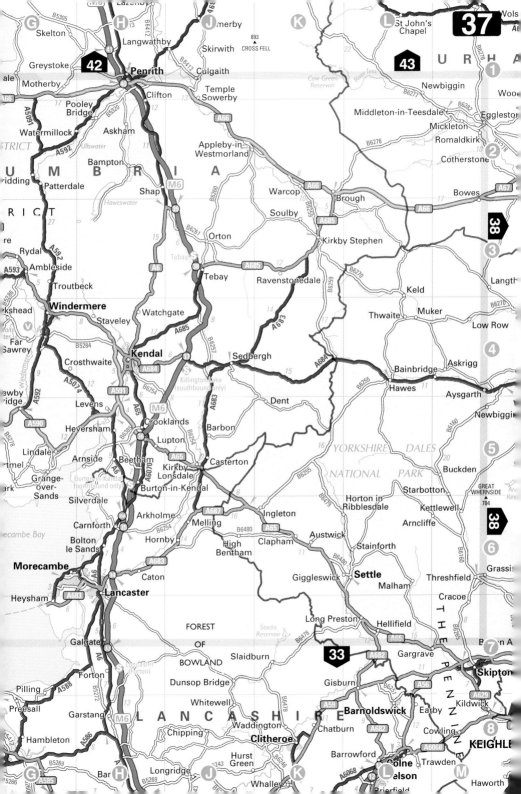

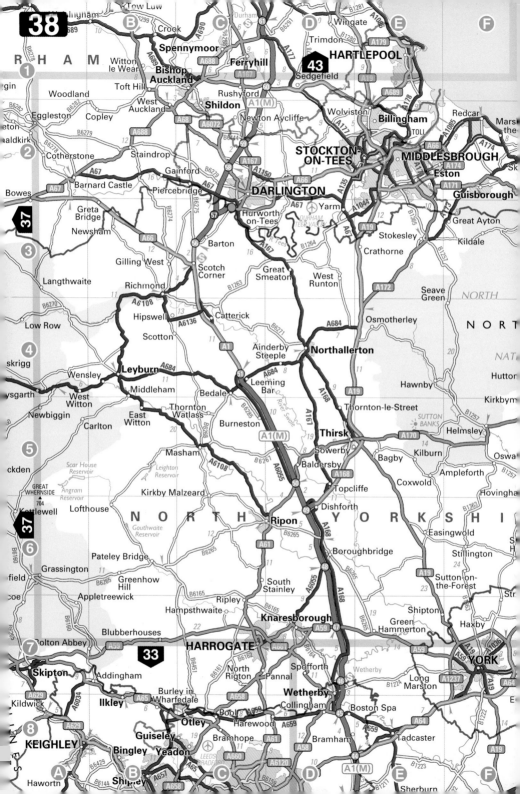

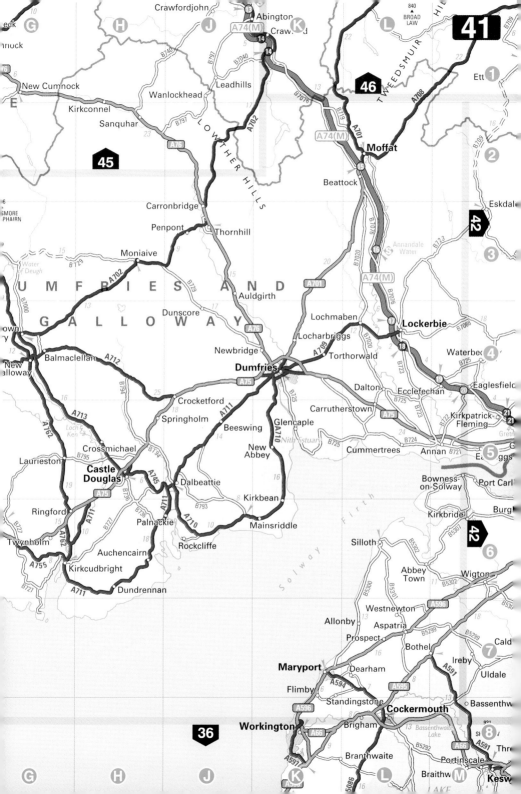

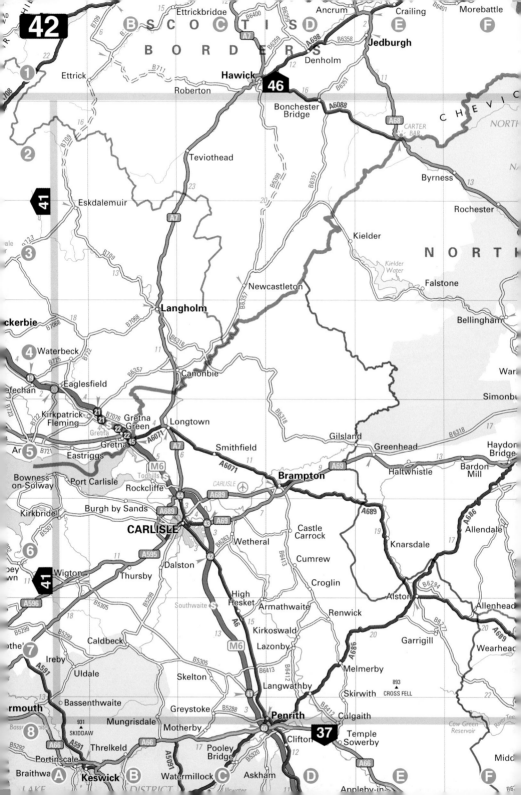

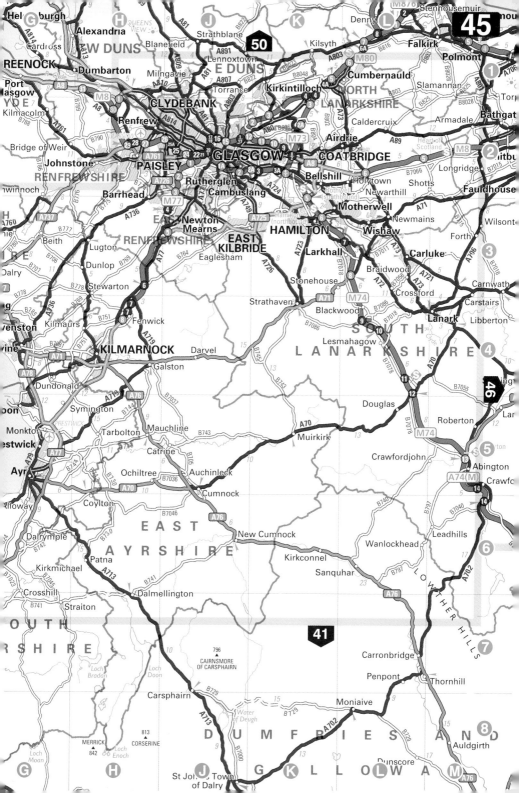

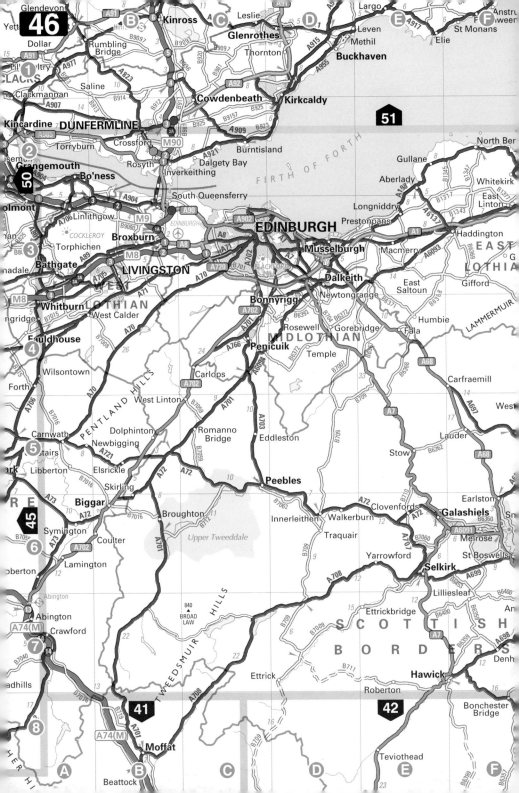

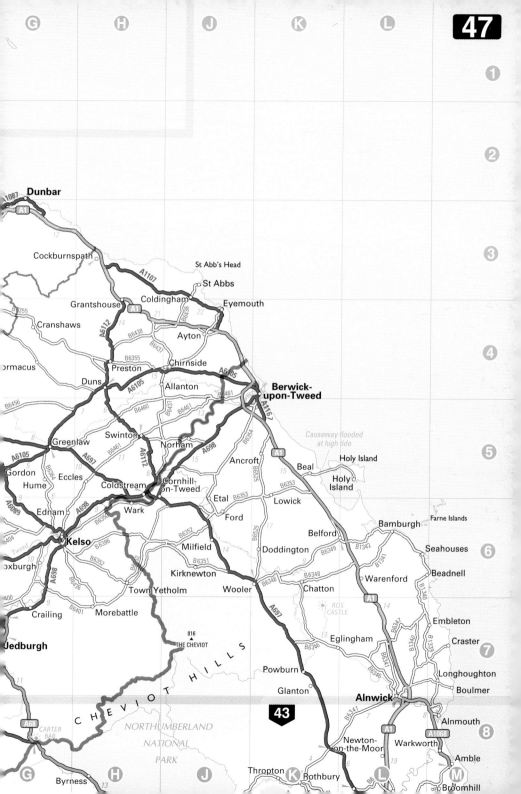

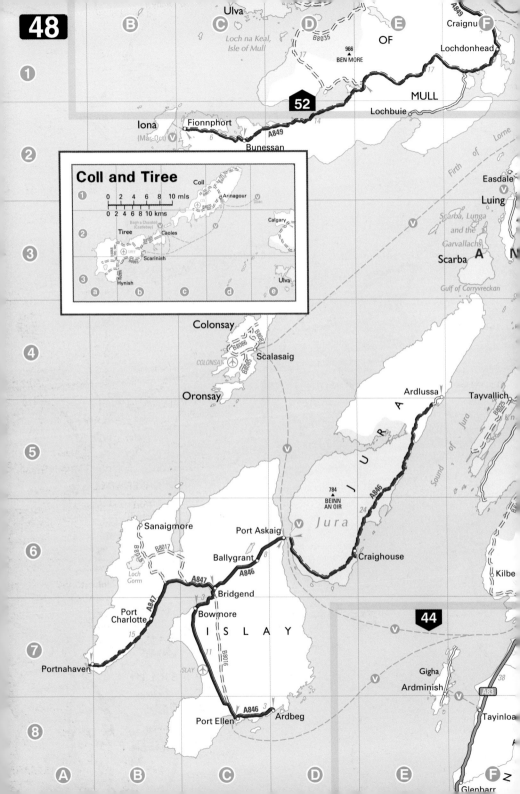

48

Ulva
Loch na Keal,
Isle of Mull
B8035
OF
Craignu
A849
F
Lochdonhead
966 ▲
BEN MORE
17
MULL
1
52
17
Lochbuie
Iona
(Mar-Oct) Ⓥ
Fionnphort
A849
14
2
Bunessan

Coll and Tiree

Coll
0 2 4 6 8 10 mls
Arinagour
Oban Ⓥ
0 2 4 6 8 10 kms
Tiree
Caoles
Calgary
B8065
Scarinish
Ulva
Hynish
a
b
c
d
e

Easdale
Luing
Ⓥ
Scarba, Lunga
and the
Garvallachs
Scarba
A
N

Colonsay
B8086
B8087
Scalasaig
4
COLONSAY
Gulf of Corryvreckan

Oronsay
Ardlussa
Tayvallich
B8025
Ⓥ
Ⓥ
JURA
5
784 ▲
BEINN
AN OIR
Jura
24
A846
Sound of Jura

Sanaigmore
Port Askaig
B8017
Ⓥ
6
B8018
Ballygrant
8
Craighouse
A847
A846
Kilbe
Loch
Bridgend
Gorm
3
Port
Charlotte
Bowmore
44
A847
ISLAY
Ⓥ
7
15
B8016
Gigha
11
Ardminish
A83
Portnahaven
SLAY
Ⓥ
Tayinloa
Ⓥ
A846
3
Ardbeg
8
Port Ellen
F
Glenbarr

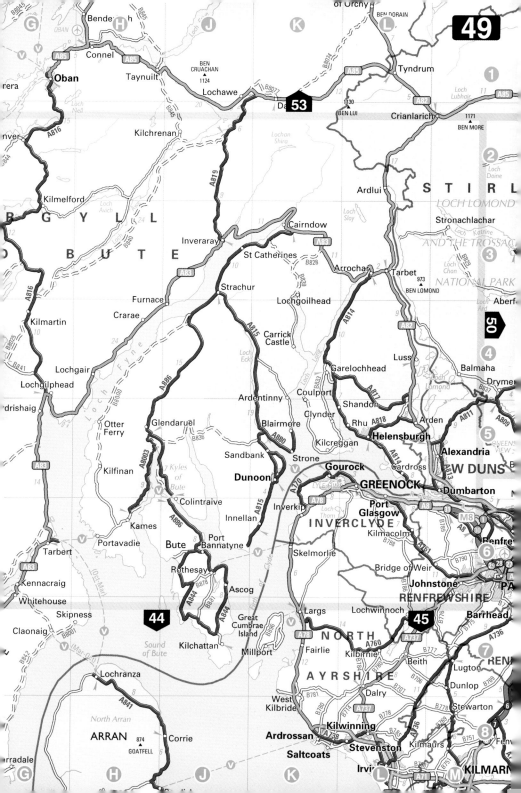

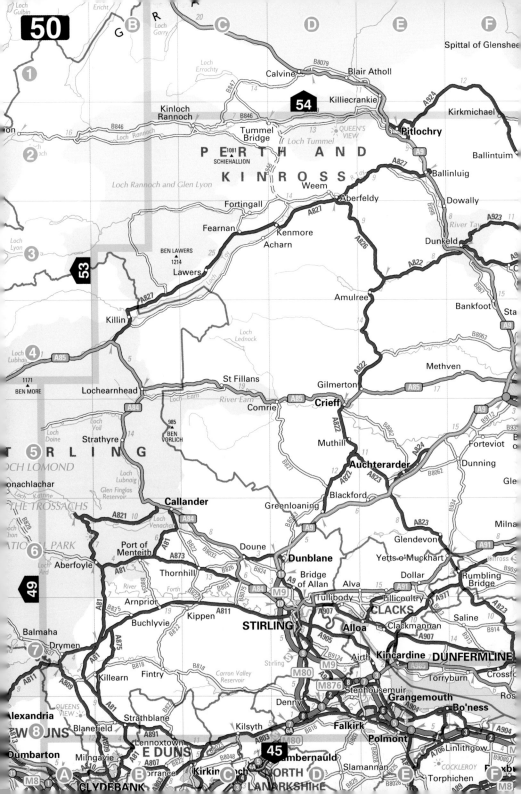

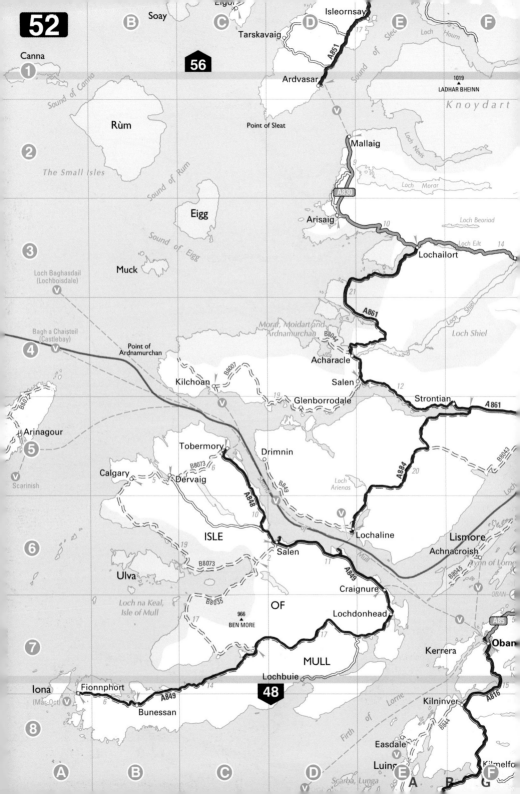

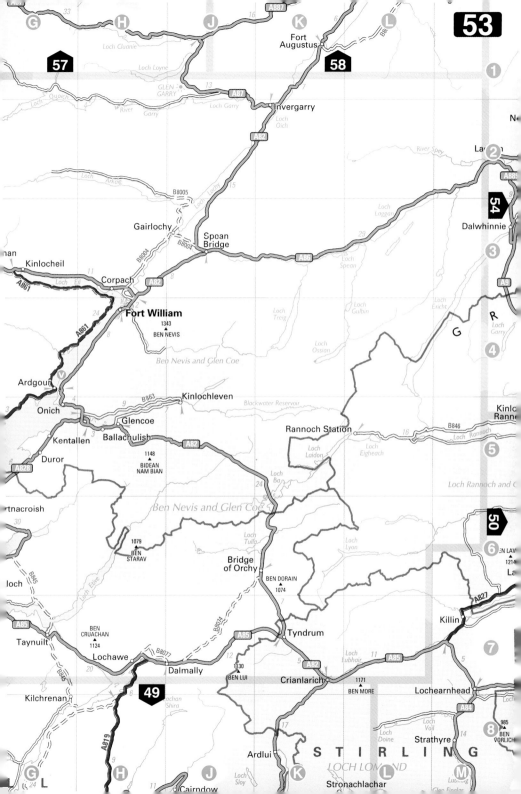

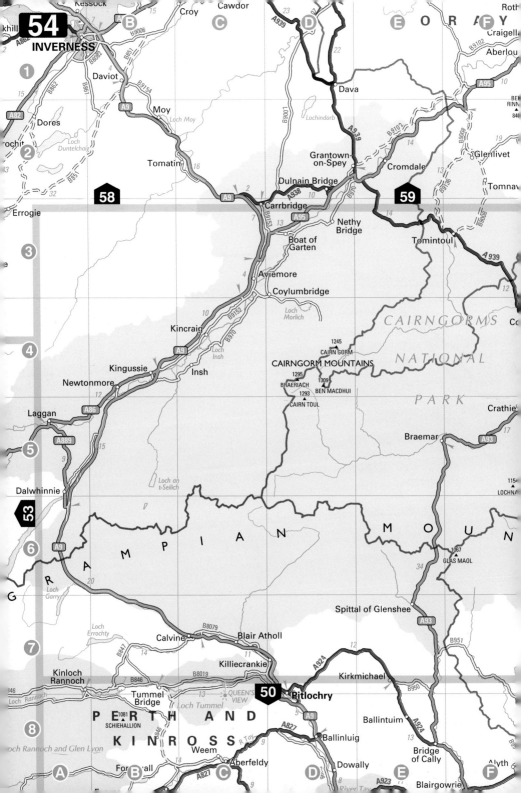

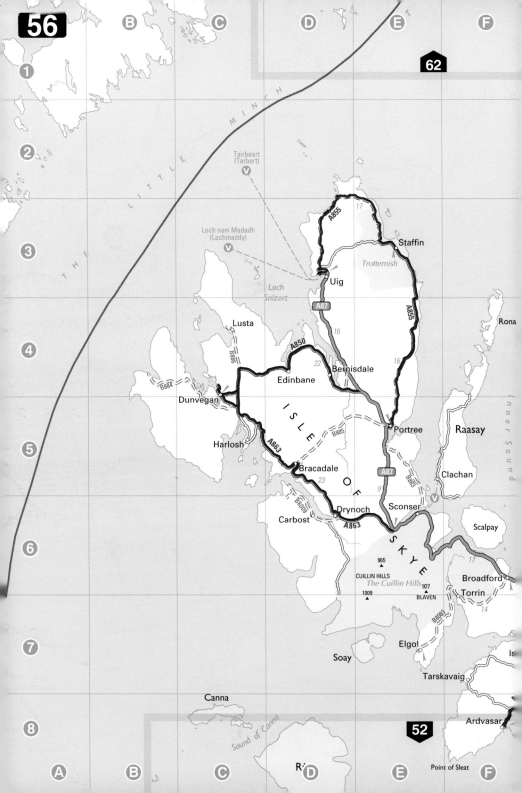

THE LITTLE MINCH

Tairbeart
(Tarbert)

Loch nam Madadh
(Lochmaddy)

62

A855

17

Staffin

Trotternish

Uig

Loch
Snizort

A87

Lusta

16

B886

A850

22

Bernisdale

16

Rona

Edinbane

ISLE

Dunvegan

B884

Harlosh

A863

B885

Portree

Raasay

Inner Sound

O F

Bracadale

A87

Clachan

23

9

B883

Drynoch

Sconser

Carbost

B8009

A863

SKYE

Scalpay

965
CUILLIN HILLS
The Cuillin Hills   927
1009   BLAVEN

Broadford

Torrin

Soay

Elgol

B8083

14

Tarskavaig

Is

Canna

Sound of Canna

R

52

Ardvasar

Point of Sleat

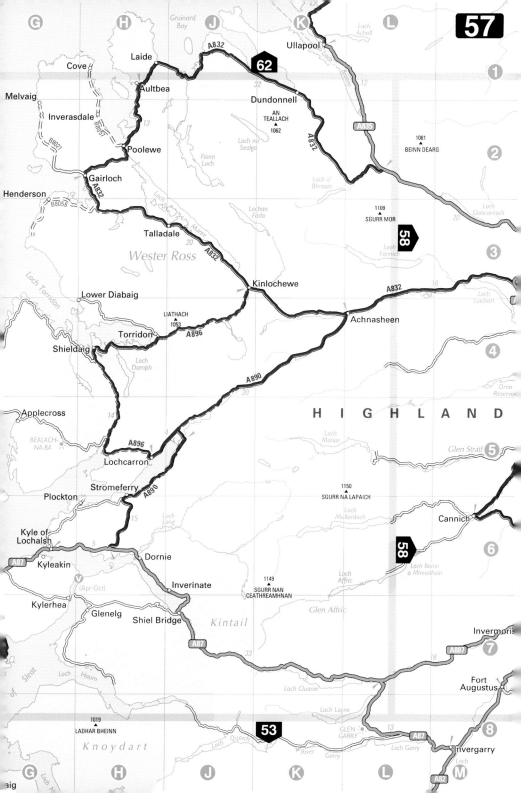

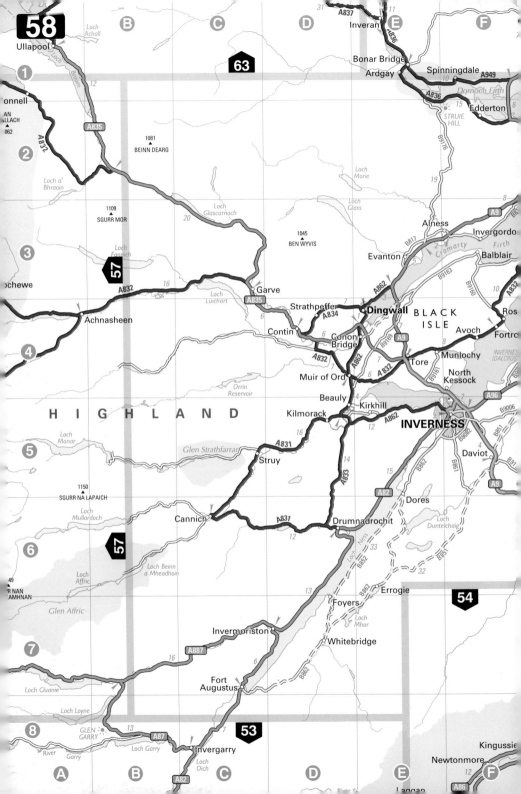

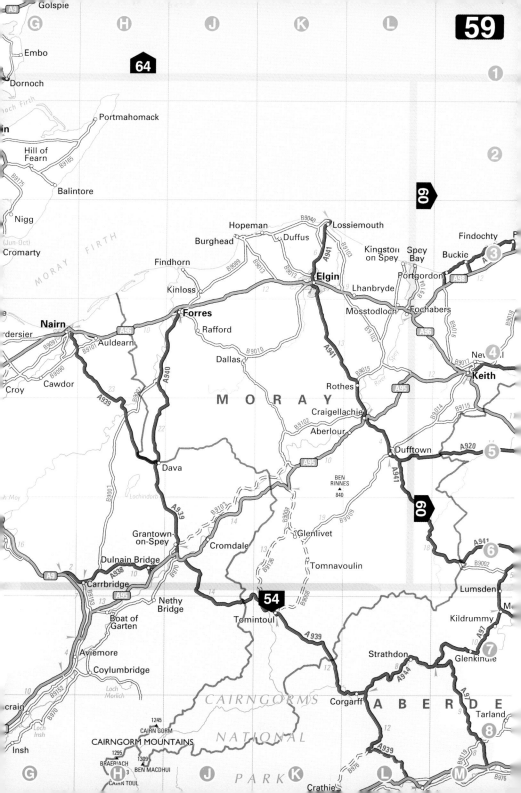

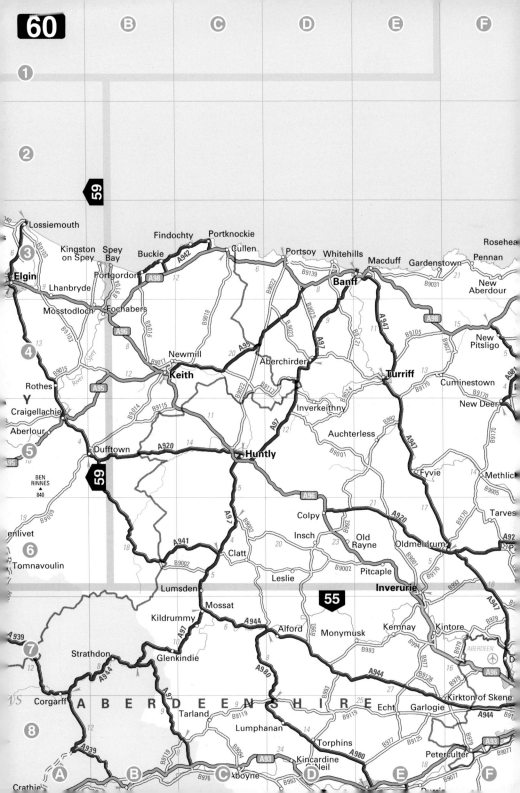

B   C   D   E   F

1

2

59

Lossiemouth

Findochty   Portknockie
Kingston   Spey   Buckie   Cullen   Portsoy   Whitehills   Roseheal
on Spey   Bay   A942   Macduff   Gardenstown   Pennan
Portgordon   A98   B9139   Banff   New Aberdour
Elgin   A98   B9031
Lhanbryde   B9022   B9025   A98   New Pitsligo
Mosstodloch   Fochabers   A96   B9018   9   11   A941   B9105   15
Newmill   A95   20   Aberchirder   A97   Turriff   Cuminestown   New Deer
Keith   B9024   13   B9170
Rothes   A95   B9022   B9117   Inverkeithny   New Deer
Craigellachie   B9014   B9115   11   Auchterless   B992   A947   Methlick
Aberlour   A97   12   B9001   Fyvie   14
Dufftown   A920   14   Huntly   Tarves
95   BEN   59   5   A96   A92
RINNES   840   Colpy   A920   17   B9170
19   B9009   Insch   Old   23   Oldmeldrum
Tomnavoulin   6   18   Clatt   20   Rayne   B9002   Pitcaple
enlivet   A941   5   Leslie   Inverurie   A947
Lumsden   B9002   55
Mossat   A947
Kildrummy   A944   Alford   Monymusk   Kemnay   Kintore   B979
7   Strathdon   A97   10   B993   ABERDEEN   A96
Glenkindie   A980   8   A944   16   D
Corgarff   A939   A944   A B E R D E E N S H I R E   25   Kirkton of Skene   A944
Tarland   B9119   Echt   Garlogie   A93
8   Lumphanan   14   Torphins   B977   B9125   B979   Peterculter
A939   12   B9119   8   A980   24   Kincardine   A93
Crathie   B976   Aboyne   O'Neil   B9077

A   B   C   D   E   F

G   H   J   K   L

① ② ③ ④ ⑤ ⑥ ⑦ ⑧

Sandhaven

Fraserburgh

Inverallochy

B9033

emsie   A90   St Combs

Rathen

Crimond

Strichen   A952

St Fergus

Mintlaw   PETERHEAD Ⓗ

d Deer   A950   **Peterhead**

Longside

rtfield

Clola   A952   Boddam

Hatton   A90

Cruden Bay

A975

Collieston

Newburgh

A975

Balmedie

A90

Ⓥ Kirkwall Lerwick

ABERDEEN

Shetland Islands

```
0      5      10     15 mls   Herma Ness
|   |   |   |   |   |   |
0   5   10   15   20 kms
```

①   Haroldswick

Unst   A968   Baltasound

Ⓥ   Uyeasound

②   Gutcher

Yell   Mid Yell   Fetlar

West Sandwick   A968

③   Ollaberry   Ulsta   Burravoe

B9078   Out Skerries

Hillswick   Toft

SHETLAND

Brae   Vidlin

④   Muckle Roe   Voe   Ⓥ   Whalsay

Sandness   **ISLANDS**   Symbister

A971

⑤   Walls   A970

Scalloway   **Lerwick**

⑥   Kirkabister

MAINLAND   Bressay

A970   Fladdabister

⑦   Sandwick

Ⓥ Kirkwall Aberdeen

⑧   SUMBURGH

Sumburgh Head

ⓐ ⓑ ⓒ ⓓ ⓔ

G   H   J   K   L   M

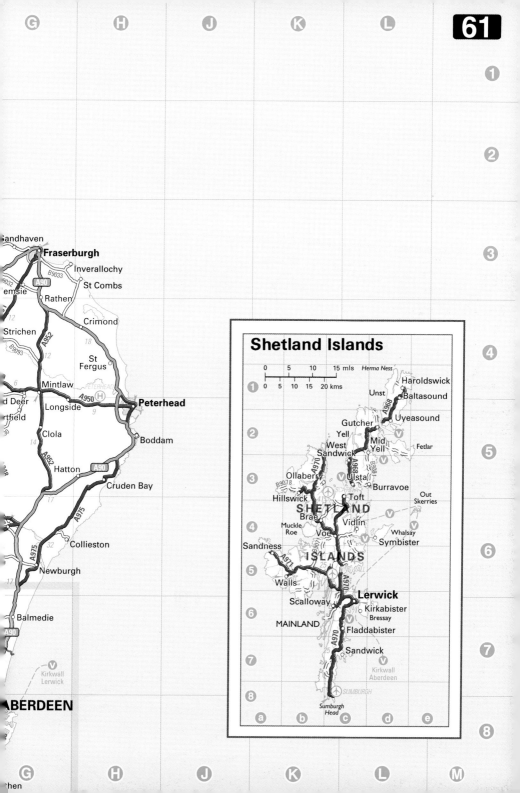

Western Isles

0   5   10   15   20 mls
0   5 10 15 20 25 kms

Rudha Rhobhanais
(Butt of Lewis)
Port Nis
(Port of Ness)
A857
Barabhas
(Barvas)
Tolastadh
(Tolsta)
Carlabhagh
(Carloway)
A857
B895
Miabhig
(Miavaig)
Breascleit
(Breasclete)
A858
B866
STORNOWAY
Steornabhagh
(Stornoway)
ISLE OF LEWIS
Baile Ailein
(Balallan)
B8011
A859
South Lewis,
Harris and North Uist
B8060
NA H-EILEANAN
CLISHAM
799
B887
Ullapool
AN IAR
Taransay
Tairbeart
(Tarbert)
A859
Scalpay
HARRIS
Pabbay
An t-Ob
(Leverburgh)
Berneray
Tigh a
Ghearraidh
(Tigharry)
A865
B893
Loch nam
Madadh
(Lochmaddy)
J
UIBHIST A
TUATH
(North Uist)
A867
BENBECULA
Uig
Baile a
Mhanaich
(Balivanich)
BEINN NA
FAOGHLA
(Benbecula)
i
Creag Ghoraidh
(Creagorry)
ISLE
OF SKYE
B890
Stadhlaigearraidh
(Stilligarry)
A865
h
UIBHIST A
DEAS
(South Uist)
B888
Loch Baghasdail
(Lochboisdale)
Barraigh
(Barra)
Eriskay
Oban
g
BARRA
A888
Bagh a Chaisteil
(Castlebay)
Vatersay
Oban
Coll & Tiree
(Mar-Oct)
f

a   b   c   d   e

56

Altandhu
Steornabhagh
(Stornoway)
Ac

THE MINCH

Gruinard
Bay
Laide
A832
Cove
Aultbea
57
32
Du
Melvaig
Inverasdale
B802
Loch na
Sealg

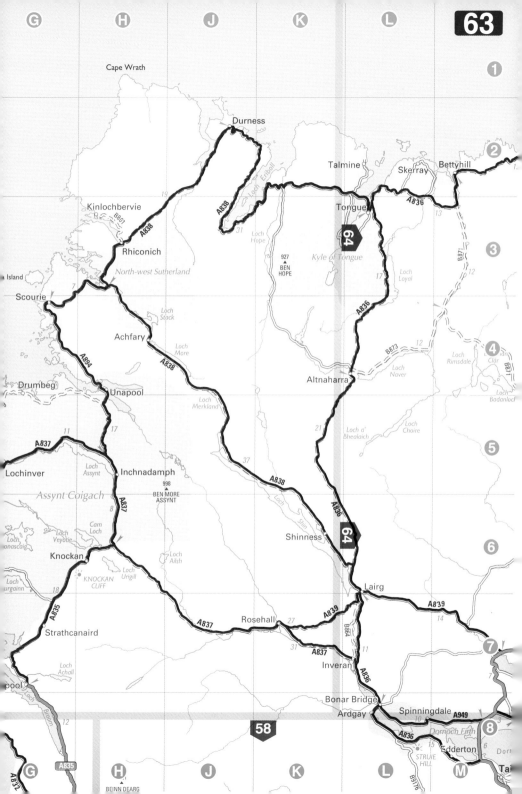

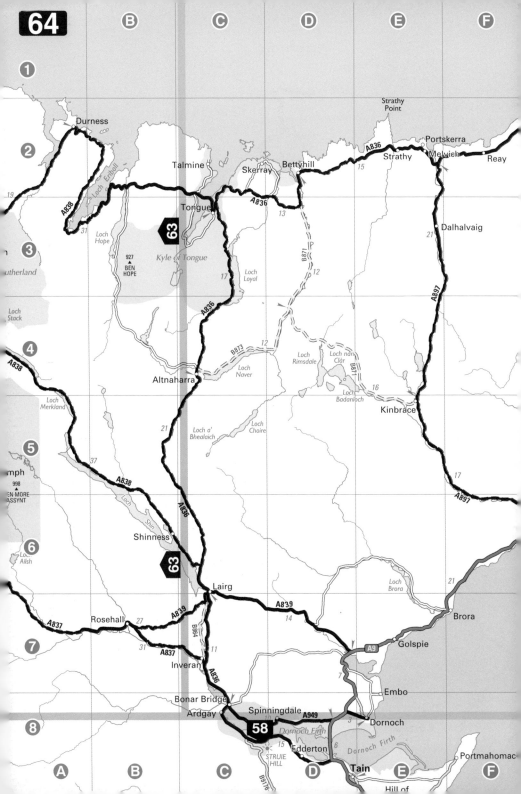

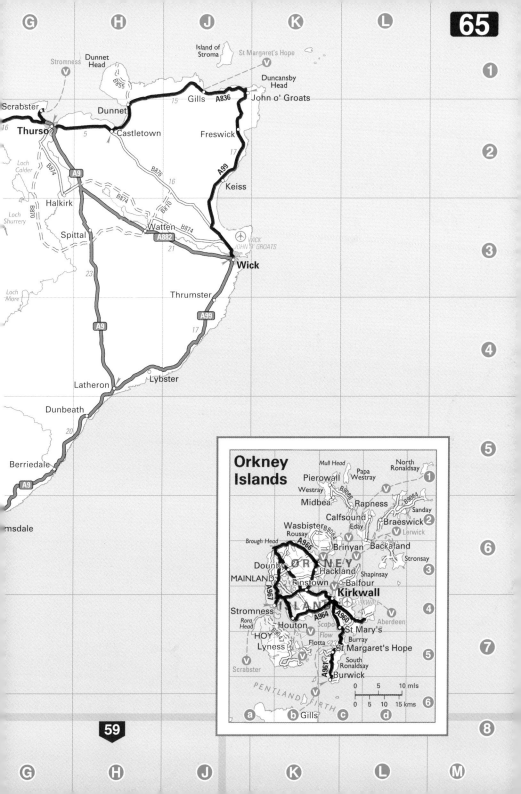

Index to places in Britain

This index lists places appearing in the main-map section of the atlas in alphabetical order. The reference following each name gives the atlas page number and grid reference of the square in which the place appears. The map shows counties, unitary authorities and administrative areas, together with a list of the abbreviated name forms used in the index.

England

BaNES	**Bath & N E Somerset (18)**
Barns	**Barnsley (19)**
Bed	**Bedford**
Birm	**Birmingham**
Bl w D	**Blackburn with Darwen (20)**
Bmouth	**Bournemouth**
Bolton	**Bolton (21)**
Bpool	**Blackpool**
Br & H	**Brighton & Hove (22)**
Br For	**Bracknell Forest (23)**
Bristl	**City of Bristol**
Bucks	**Buckinghamshire**
Bury	**Bury (24)**
C Beds	**Central Bedfordshire**
C Brad	**City of Bradford**
C Derb	**City of Derby**
C KuH	**City of Kingston upon Hull**
C Leic	**City of Leicester**
C Nott	**City of Nottingham**
C Pete	**City of Peterborough**
C Plym	**City of Plymouth**
C Port	**City of Portsmouth**
C Sotn	**City of Southampton**
C Stke	**City of Stoke-on-Trent**
C York	**City of York**
Calder	**Calderdale (25)**
Cambs	**Cambridgeshire**
Ches E	**Cheshire East**
Ches W	**Cheshire West and Chester**
Cnwll	**Cornwall**
Covtry	**Coventry**
Cumb	**Cumbria**
Darltn	**Darlington (26)**
Derbys	**Derbyshire**
Devon	**Devon**
Donc	**Doncaster (27)**
Dorset	**Dorset**
Dudley	**Dudley (28)**
Dur	**Durham**
E R Yk	**East Riding of Yorkshire**
E Susx	**East Sussex**
Essex	**Essex**
Gatesd	**Gateshead (29)**
Gloucs	**Gloucestershire**
Gt Lon	**Greater London**
Halton	**Halton (30)**
Hants	**Hampshire**
Hartpl	**Hartlepool (31)**
Herefs	**Herefordshire**
Herts	**Hertfordshire**
IoS	**Isles of Scilly**
IoW	**Isle of Wight**
Kent	**Kent**
Kirk	**Kirklees (32)**
Knows	**Knowsley (33)**
Lancs	**Lancashire**
Leeds	**Leeds**
Leics	**Leicestershire**
Lincs	**Lincolnshire**
Lpool	**Liverpool**
Luton	**Luton**
M Keyn	**Milton Keynes**
Manch	**Manchester**
Medway	**Medway**
Middsb	**Middlesbrough**
NE Lin	**North East Lincolnshire**
N Linc	**North Lincolnshire**
N Som	**North Somerset (34)**
N Tyne	**North Tyneside (35)**
N u Ty	**Newcastle upon Tyne**
N York	**North Yorkshire**
Nhants	**Northamptonshire**
Norfk	**Norfolk**
Notts	**Nottinghamshire**
Nthumb	**Northumberland**
Oldham	**Oldham (36)**
Oxon	**Oxfordshire**
Poole	**Poole**
R & Cl	**Redcar & Cleveland**
Readg	**Reading**
Rochdl	**Rochdale (37)**
Rothm	**Rotherham (38)**
Rutlnd	**Rutland**
S Glos	**South Gloucestershire (39)**
S on T	**Stockton-on-Tees (40)**
S Tyne	**South Tyneside (41)**
Salfd	**Salford (42)**
Sandw	**Sandwell (43)**
Sefton	**Sefton (44)**
Sheff	**Sheffield**
Shrops	**Shropshire**
Slough	**Slough (45)**
Solhll	**Solihull (46)**
Somset	**Somerset**
St Hel	**St Helens (47)**
Staffs	**Staffordshire**
Sthend	**Southend-on-Sea**
Stockp	**Stockport (48)**
Suffk	**Suffolk**
Sundld	**Sunderland**
Surrey	**Surrey**
Swindn	**Swindon**
Tamesd	**Tameside (49)**
Thurr	**Thurrock (50)**
Torbay	**Torbay**
Traffd	**Trafford (51)**
W & M	**Windsor and Maidenhead (52)**
W Berk	**West Berkshire**
W Susx	**West Sussex**
Wakefd	**Wakefield (53)**
Warrtn	**Warrington (54)**
Warwks	**Warwickshire**
Wigan	**Wigan (55)**
Wilts	**Wiltshire**
Wirral	**Wirral (56)**
Wokham	**Wokingham (57)**
Wolves	**Wolverhampton (58)**
Worcs	**Worcestershire**
Wrekin	**Telford & Wrekin (59)**
Wsall	**Walsall (60)**

Channel Islands & Isle of Man

Guern	**Guernsey**
Jersey	**Jersey**
IoM	**Isle of Man**

Scotland

Abers	**Aberdeenshire**
Ag & B	**Argyll and Bute**
Angus	**Angus**
Border	**Scottish Borders**
C Aber	**City of Aberdeen**
C Dund	**City of Dundee**
C Edin	**City of Edinburgh**
C Glas	**City of Glasgow**
Clacks	**Clackmannanshire (1)**
D & G	**Dumfries & Galloway**
E Ayrs	**East Ayrshire**
E Duns	**East Dunbartonshire (2)**
E Loth	**East Lothian**
E Rens	**East Renfrewshire (3)**
Falk	**Falkirk**
Fife	**Fife**
Highld	**Highland**
Inver	**Inverclyde (4)**
Mdloth	**Midlothian (5)**
Moray	**Moray**
N Ayrs	**North Ayrshire**
N Lans	**North Lanarkshire (6)**
Ork	**Orkney Islands**
P & K	**Perth & Kinross**
Rens	**Renfrewshire (7)**
S Ayrs	**South Ayrshire**
Shet	**Shetland Islands**
S Lans	**South Lanarkshire**
Stirlg	**Stirling**
W Duns	**West Dunbartonshire (8)**
W Isls	**Western Isles (Na h-Eileanan an Iar)**
W Loth	**West Lothian**

Wales

Blae G	**Blaenau Gwent (9)**
Brdgnd	**Bridgend (10)**
Caerph	**Caerphilly (11)**
Cardif	**Cardiff**
Carmth	**Carmarthenshire**
Cerdgn	**Ceredigion**
Conwy	**Conwy**
Denbgs	**Denbighshire**
Flints	**Flintshire**
Gwynd	**Gwynedd**
IoA	**Isle of Anglesey**
Mons	**Monmouthshire**
Myr Td	**Merthyr Tydfil (12)**
Neath	**Neath Port Talbot (13)**
Newpt	**Newport (14)**
Pembks	**Pembrokeshire**
Powys	**Powys**
Rhondd	**Rhondda Cynon Taff (15)**
Swans	**Swansea**
Torfn	**Torfaen (16)**
V Glam	**Vale of Glamorgan (17)**
Wrexhm	**Wrexham**

Distance chart - Britain

This chart shows distances in miles between two towns along AA-recommended routes. Using motorways and other main roads this is normally the fastest route, though not necessarily the shortest.

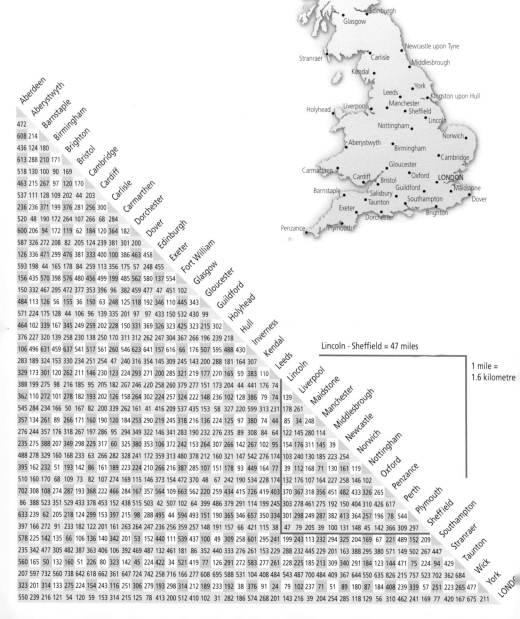

Lincoln - Sheffield = 47 miles

1 mile = 1.6 kilometre

Cities (diagonal labels, in order): Aberdeen, Aberystwyth, Barnstaple, Birmingham, Brighton, Bristol, Cambridge, Cardiff, Carlisle, Carmarthen, Dorchester, Dover, Edinburgh, Exeter, Fort William, Glasgow, Gloucester, Guildford, Holyhead, Hull, Inverness, Kendal, Leeds, Lincoln, Liverpool, Maidstone, Manchester, Middlesbrough, Newcastle, Norwich, Nottingham, Oxford, Penzance, Perth, Plymouth, Sheffield, Southampton, Stranraer, Taunton, Wick, York, LONDON

```
472
608 214
436 124 180
613 288 210 171
518 130 100 90 169
463 215 267 97 120 170
537 111 128 109 202 44 203
236 336 371 199 376 281 256 300
520 48 190 172 264 107 266 68 284
600 206 94 172 119 62 184 120 364 182
587 326 272 208 82 205 124 239 381 301 200
126 336 471 299 476 381 400 100 386 463 458
593 198 44 165 178 84 259 113 356 175 57 248 455
156 435 570 398 576 480 456 499 199 485 562 580 137 554
150 332 467 295 472 377 353 396 96 382 459 477 47 451 102
484 113 126 56 155 36 150 63 248 125 118 192 346 110 445 343
571 224 175 128 44 106 96 139 335 201 97 97 433 150 532 430 99
464 102 339 167 345 249 259 202 228 150 331 369 326 323 425 323 215 302
376 227 320 139 258 230 138 250 170 311 312 262 247 304 367 266 196 239 218
106 496 631 459 637 541 517 561 260 546 623 641 157 616 66 176 507 595 488 430
283 189 324 153 330 234 251 254 47 240 316 354 309 245 143 200 288 181 164 307
329 173 301 120 262 211 146 230 123 224 293 271 200 285 321 219 177 220 165 59 383 110
388 199 275 98 216 185 95 205 182 267 246 220 258 260 379 277 151 173 204 44 441 176 74
362 110 272 101 278 182 193 202 126 158 264 302 224 257 324 222 148 236 102 128 386 79 74 139
545 284 234 166 50 167 82 200 339 262 161 41 416 209 537 435 153 58 327 220 599 313 231 178 261
357 134 261 89 266 171 190 190 184 253 290 219 245 318 216 136 224 125 97 380 74 44 85 34 248
276 244 357 176 318 267 197 286 95 294 349 322 146 341 283 190 232 276 235 89 308 84 64 122 145 280 114
235 275 388 207 349 298 229 317 60 325 380 353 106 372 242 153 264 307 266 142 267 102 95 154 176 311 145 39
488 278 329 160 168 233 63 266 282 328 241 172 359 313 480 378 212 160 321 147 542 276 174 103 240 130 185 223 254
395 162 232 51 193 142 86 161 189 223 224 210 266 216 387 285 107 151 178 93 449 164 77 39 112 168 71 130 161 119
510 160 170 68 109 73 82 107 274 169 115 146 373 154 472 370 48 67 242 190 534 228 174 132 176 107 164 227 258 146 102
702 308 108 274 287 193 368 222 466 284 167 357 564 109 663 562 220 259 434 415 726 419 403 370 367 318 356 451 482 433 326 265
86 388 523 351 529 433 378 453 152 438 515 503 42 507 102 64 399 486 379 291 114 199 245 303 278 461 275 192 150 404 310 426 617
633 239 62 205 218 124 299 153 397 215 98 288 495 44 594 493 151 190 365 346 657 350 334 301 298 249 287 382 413 364 257 196 78 544
397 166 272 91 233 182 122 201 161 263 264 247 236 256 359 257 148 191 157 66 421 115 38 47 79 205 39 100 131 148 45 142 366 309 297
578 225 142 135 66 106 136 140 342 201 53 152 440 111 539 437 100 49 309 258 601 295 241 199 243 113 232 294 325 204 169 67 221 489 152 209
235 342 477 305 482 387 363 406 106 392 469 487 132 461 181 86 352 440 333 276 261 153 229 288 232 445 229 201 163 388 295 380 571 149 502 267 447
560 165 50 132 160 51 226 80 323 142 45 224 422 34 521 419 77 126 291 272 583 277 261 228 225 185 213 309 340 291 184 123 144 471 75 224 94 429
207 597 732 560 738 642 618 662 361 647 724 742 258 716 166 277 608 695 588 531 104 408 484 543 487 700 484 409 367 644 550 635 826 215 757 523 702 362 684
323 201 314 133 275 224 154 243 156 251 306 279 193 298 314 212 189 233 192 38 376 91 24 79 102 237 71 51 89 180 87 184 408 239 339 57 251 223 265 477
550 239 216 121 54 120 59 153 314 215 125 78 413 200 512 410 102 31 282 186 574 268 201 143 216 39 204 254 285 118 129 56 310 462 241 169 77 420 167 675 211
```

A

Abberley Worcs 21 L4
Abbey Town Cumb 41 L6
Abbots Bromley
  Staffs 29 H7
Aberaeron Cerdgn 19 H1
Aberarth Cerdgn 19 H1
Aberchirder Abers 60 D4
Aberdare Rhondd 12 B2
Aberdaron Gwynd 26 B6
Aberdeen C Aber 55 M4
Aberdyfi Gwynd 20 A2
Aberfeldy P & K 50 D2
Aberffraw IoA 26 C3
Aberfoyle Stirlg 50 B6
Abergavenny Mons 21 C8
Abergele Conwy 27 H3
Aberlady E Loth 46 E2
Aberlour Moray 59 L5
Abermule Powys 20 F2
Abernethy P & K 51 G5
Aberporth Cerdgn 18 F2
Abersoch Gwynd 26 C6
Abersychan Torfn 12 D2
Abertillery Blae G 12 D2
Aberystwyth Cerdgn .. 20 A3
Abingdon-on-
  Thames Oxon 14 C4
Abington S Lans 45 M6
Ab Kettleby Leics 30 D7
Aboyne Abers 55 J4
Abridge Essex 16 D7
Accrington Lancs 33 G4
Acharacle Highld 52 D4
Acharn P & K 50 C3
Achfary Highld 63 H4
Achiltibuie Highld 62 F6
Achnacroish Ag & B ... 52 F6
Achnasheen Highld 57 L4
Ackworth Moor Top
  Wakefd 34 B5
Acle Norfk 25 K5
Acton Trussell Staffs .. 29 G7
Addingham C Brad 33 J2
Adwick Le Street
  Donc 34 C6
Ainderby Steeple
  N York 38 D4
Airdrie N Lans 45 L2
Airth Falk 50 E7
Albrighton Shrops 21 L1
Albrighton Shrops 28 C7
Albury Surrey 9 K2
Alcester Warwks 22 B4
Alconbury Cambs 23 M3
Aldbourne Wilts 14 A6
Aldbrough E R Yk 35 J3
Aldeburgh Suffk 17 M2
Alderbury Wilts 8 C3
Alderley Edge Ches E .. 28 F3
Aldermaston W Berk ... 14 D7
Alderminster Warwks .. 22 D5
Aldershot Hants 9 H2
Aldford Ches W 28 B4
Aldham Essex 17 G5
Aldsworth Gloucs 13 L1
Alexandria W Duns 49 M5
Alfold Surrey 9 K3
Alford Abers 55 J3
Alford Lincs 31 K3
Alfreton Derbys 29 L4
Alfriston E Susx 10 D7
Alkham Kent 11 K4
Allanton Border 47 H4
Allendale Nthumb 42 F6
Allenheads Nthumb 42 F7
Allensmore Herefs 21 J6
Alloa Clacks 50 E7
Allonby Cumb 41 J6
Alloway S Ayrs 45 G6
Almondsbury S Glos .. 13 G3
Alness Highld 58 F3
Alnmouth Nthumb 43 L4
Alnwick Nthumb 47 L7
Alrewas Staffs 29 J7
Alsager Ches E 28 E4
Alston Cumb 42 E6
Altandhu Highld 62 F6
Althorpe N Linc 34 E5
Altnaharra Highld 64 C4
Alton Hants 9 H2
Alton Pancras Dorset .. 7 K2
Altrincham Traffd 28 F3
Alva Clacks 50 E6
Alveston S Glos 13 G3
Alyth P & K 51 G3
Amberley W Susx 9 K4
Amble Nthumb 43 K2
Ambleside Cumb 37 G3

Amersham Bucks 15 G4
Amesbury Wilts 8 C2
Amlwch IoA 26 D1
Ammanford Carmth ... 19 J5
Ampleforth N York 38 F5
Ampthill C Beds 23 K6
Amroth Pembks 18 E5
Amulree P & K 50 E3
Ancaster Lincs 30 F5
Ancroft Nthumb 47 K5
Ancrum Border 47 G7
Andover Hants 8 D2
Andoversford Gloucs .. 22 B7
Andreas IoM 36 c1
Angle Pembks 18 C6
Angmering W Susx 9 K5
Annan D & G 41 M5
Annfield Plain Dur 43 J6
Anstey Leics 30 C8
Anstruther Fife 51 K6
An t-Ob W Isls 62 e7
Anwick Lincs 31 G5
Appleby-in-
  Westmorland
  Cumb 37 J2
Applecross Highld 57 G3
Appledore Devon 4 D4
Appledore Kent 11 H5
Appletreewick
  N York 38 A7
Arbroath Angus 51 L3
Arclid Green Ches E .. 28 E4
Ardbeg Ag & B 48 D8
Arden Ag & B 49 L5
Ardentinny Ag & B 49 K4
Ardersier Highld 59 G4
Ardgay Highld 64 C8
Ardgour Highld 53 G4
Ardingly W Susx 10 C5
Ardleigh Essex 17 H4
Ardlui Ag & B 49 L2
Ardlussa Ag & B 48 E4
Ardminish Ag & B 44 A3
Ardrishaig Ag & B 49 G5
Ardrossan N Ayrs 44 F4
Ardwell D & G 40 C7
Arinagour Ag & B 48 d1
Arisaig Highld 52 D3
Arkholme Lancs 37 J6
Armadale W Loth 45 M2
Armathwaite Cumb 42 C7
Arncliffe N York 37 M6
Arnprior Stirlg 50 B7
Arnside Cumb 37 H5
Arrington Cambs 16 B3
Arrochar Ag & B 49 L3
Arundel W Susx 9 K5
Ascog Ag & B 49 J6
Ascot W & M 15 G6
Ash Kent 11 K3
Ashbourne Derbys 29 J5
Ashburton Devon 6 B5
Ashbury Oxon 14 A5
Ashby-de-la-Zouch
  Leics 29 K7
Ashcott Somset 12 E7
Ashford Kent 11 H4
Ashington Nthumb 43 K3
Ashington W Susx 9 L4
Ashley Cambs 16 E2
Ashton-under-Lyne
  Tamesd 33 H6
Ashurst Hants 8 D5
Ashwater Devon 4 D7
Askam in Furness
  Cumb 36 F5
Askern Donc 34 C5
Askham Cumb 37 H2
Askrigg N York 37 M4
Aspatria Cumb 41 L7
Aston Oxon 14 B4
Aston Clinton Bucks .. 14 F3
Aston on Clun Shrops .. 21 H3
Aston Rowant Oxon ... 14 E4
Atcham Shrops 28 C8
Atherstone Warwks ... 22 D1
Atherton Wigan 32 F6
Attleborough Norfk 25 H6
Attlebridge Norfk 25 H4
Atwick E R Yk 35 H2
Auchenblae Abers 55 K6
Auchencairn D & G 41 H6
Auchinleck E Ayrs 45 J5
Auchterarder P & K ... 50 E5
Auchterless Abers 60 E5
Auchtermuchty Fife .. 51 G5
Audlem Ches E 28 D5
Audley Staffs 28 E5
Auldearn Highld 59 H4
Auldgirth D & G 41 J3

Aultbea Highld 57 H1
Austwick N York 37 K6
Avebury Wilts 13 L4
Avening Gloucs 13 J2
Aveton Gifford
  Devon 6 A6
Aviemore Highld 54 C3
Avoch Highld 58 F4
Avonmouth Bristl 12 F4
Awsworth Notts 30 B5
Axbridge Somset 12 E5
Axminster Devon 6 F3
Axmouth Devon 6 F3
Aylesbury Bucks 14 F3
Aylesham Kent 11 K3
Aylsham Norfk 25 J3
Aynho Nhants 22 F6
Ayr S Ayrs 45 G5
Aysgarth N York 38 A4
Ayton Border 47 J4

B

Backaland Ork 65 d2
Bacton Norfk 25 K3
Bacup Lancs 33 H4
Bagby N York 38 E5
Bagh a Chaisteil
  W Isls 62 b14
Bagillt Flints 27 K3
Baglan Neath 19 K6
Bagshot Surrey 14 F7
Baile Ailein W Isls 62 g4
Baile a Mhanaich
  W Isls 62 c10
Bainbridge N York 37 M4
Bainton E R Yk 34 F2
Bakewell Derbys 29 J3
Bala Gwynd 27 H6
Balallan W Isls 62 g4
Balbeggie P & K 51 G4
Balblair Highld 58 F3
Balcombe W Susx 10 B5
Baldersby N York 38 D5
Baldock Herts 16 B4
Balfour Ork 65 C3
Balintore Highld 59 G2
Balivanich W Isls 62 c10
Ballachulish Highld ... 53 H5
Ballantrae S Ayrs 40 B4
Ballasalla IoM 36 b4
Ballater Abers 55 G5
Ballaugh IoM 36 c2
Ballinluig P & K 50 F2
Ballintuim P & K 50 F2
Ballygrant Ag & B 48 C6
Balmaclellan D & G ... 41 G4
Balmaha Stirlg 49 M4
Balmedie Abers 55 M3
Balsall Common
  Solhll 22 D3
Balsham Cambs 16 E3
Baltasound Shet 61 d1
Bamber Bridge Lancs .. 32 E4
Bamburgh Nthumb 47 L6
Bamford Derbys 29 J2
Bampton Cumb 37 H2
Bampton Devon 5 H5
Bampton Oxon 14 A4
Banbury Oxon 22 E6
Banchory Abers 55 K5
Banff Abers 60 E3
Bangor-is-y-coed
  Wrexhm 28 B5
Banham Norfk 25 H6
Bankfoot P & K 50 F4
Banstead Surrey 10 B3
Barabhas W Isls 62 h2
Barbon Cumb 37 J5
Bardney Lincs 31 G3
Bardon Mill Nthumb .. 42 F5
Bardsea Cumb 36 F5
Barford Warwks 22 D4
Bargoed Caerph 12 C2
Barking Gt Lon 16 C8
Barkston Lincs 30 F5
Barkway Herts 16 C4
Barley Herts 16 C4
Barmby Moor E R Yk .. 34 E2
Barmouth Gwynd 26 F2
Barmston E R Yk 39 L7
Barnard Castle Dur ... 38 A2
Barnby Moor Notts 30 D2
Barnet Gt Lon 15 J4
Barnetby le Wold
  N Linc 35 G6
Barnoldswick Lancs .. 33 H3
Barnsley Barns 33 M6

Barnsley Gloucs 13 L2
Barnstaple Devon 4 E4
Barr S Ayrs 40 D3
Barrasford Nthumb 43 G4
Barrhead E Rens 45 H3
Barrhill S Ayrs 40 D4
Barrowford Lancs 33 H3
Barrow-in-Furness
  Cumb 36 E6
Barrow upon Soar
  Leics 30 C7
Barry V Glam 5 K1
Barton Cambs 16 C2
Barton Lancs 32 E3
Barton N York 38 C3
Barton-le-Clay
  C Beds 23 L7
Barton Seagrave
  Nhants 23 J3
Barton-under-
  Needwood Staffs ... 29 J7
Barton-upon-
  Humber N Linc 35 G5
Barvas W Isls 62 h2
Barwell Leics 22 E2
Basildon Essex 16 F7
Basingstoke Hants 9 G1
Baslow Derbys 29 J3
Bassenthwaite
  Cumb 42 A8
Baston Lincs 31 G7
Bath BaNES 13 H5
Bathgate W Loth 46 A3
Batley Kirk 33 L4
Battle E Susx 10 F6
Baumber Lincs 31 H3
Bawdeswell Norfk 25 H4
Bawdsey Suffk 17 L4
Bawtry Donc 34 D7
Baycliff Cumb 36 F6
Bayston Hill Shrops .. 28 C8
Beaconsfield Bucks .. 15 G5
Beadnell Nthumb 47 L6
Beaford Devon 4 E4
Beal Nthumb 47 K5
Beaminster Dorset 7 H2
Beare Green Surrey 9 L2
Bearsted Kent 10 F3
Beattock D & G 41 L2
Beaulieu Hants 8 E5
Beauly Highld 58 D5
Beaumaris IoA 26 E3
Beaumont Jersey 7 b2
Beaworthy Devon 4 D7
Bebington Wirral 27 L2
Beccles Suffk 25 L6
Beckhampton Wilts ... 13 L4
Beckingham Lincs 30 E4
Beckingham Somset .. 13 H6
Beck Row Suffk 24 E7
Bedale N York 38 C4
Beddgelert Gwynd 26 E5
Bedford Bed 23 K5
Bedlington Nthumb ... 43 K4
Bedworth Warwks 22 E2
Beeford E R Yk 35 H2
Beeley Derbys 29 J3
Beer Devon 6 F3
Beesands Devon 6 B7
Beeston Ches W 28 C4
Beeston Notts 30 B6
Beeswing D & G 41 J5
Beetham Cumb 37 H5
Beetley Norfk 25 G4
Beguildy Powys 20 F3
Beith N Ayrs 45 G3
Belford Nthumb 47 L6
Bellingham Nthumb .. 42 F4
Bellochantuy Ag & B .. 44 A5
Bellshill N Lans 45 K2
Belper Derbys 29 K5
Belsay Nthumb 43 H4
Belton N Linc 34 E6
Belton Norfk 25 L5
Bembridge IoW 9 G7
Bempton E R Yk 39 L6
Benderloch Ag & B ... 52 F6
Benenden Kent 10 F5
Benllech IoA 26 D2
Benson Oxon 14 D5
Bentley Hants 9 H2
Benwick Cambs 24 B6
Bere Alston Devon 3 K4
Bere Ferrers Devon 3 K4
Bere Regis Dorset 7 L3
Berkeley Gloucs 13 G2
Berkhamsted Herts ... 15 G3
Bernisdale Highld 56 D4
Berriedale Highld 65 G5
Berriew Powys 20 F1
Berrow Somset 12 D6

Berwick St John Wilts...13 K8
Berwick-upon-
  Tweed Nthumb.......47 K4
Bethersden Kent.......11 G4
Bethesda Gwynd....26 E3
Bettyhill Highld.......64 D2
Betws-y-Coed Conwy...27 G4
Betws-yn-Rhos
  Conwy.......27 H3
Beulah Powys.......20 D5
Beverley E R Yk.......35 G3
Bewdley Worcs.......21 L3
Bexhill E Susx.......10 F7
Bibury Gloucs.......13 L1
Bicester Oxon.......14 D2
Bickleigh Devon.......5 H6
Biddenden Kent.......11 G4
Biddisham Somset.......12 E6
Biddulph Staffs.......28 F4
Bideford Devon.......4 D5
Bidford-on-Avon
  Warwks.......22 C5
Bigbury-on-Sea
  Devon.......3 M6
Biggar S Lans.......46 B6
Biggin Hill Gt Lon.......10 C3
Biggleswade C Beds...23 M5
Bildeston Suffk.......17 H3
Billericay Essex.......16 E7
Billingborough Lincs...31 G6
Billingham S on T.......38 E2
Billinghay Lincs.......31 H4
Billingshurst W Susx....9 K3
Bilsby Lincs.......31 K3
Bilsthorpe Notts.......30 C4
Binbrook Lincs.......35 H7
Binfield Br For.......14 F6
Bingham Notts.......30 D5
Bingley C Brad.......33 K3
Birdlip Gloucs.......22 A8
Birkenhead Wirral.......32 C7
Birmingham Birm.......22 B2
Birstall Leics.......30 C8
Birtley Gatesd.......43 K6
Bishop Auckland Dur...38 C1
Bishop's Castle
  Shrops.......21 G2
Bishop's Cleeve
  Gloucs.......22 A7
Bishop's Frome
  Herefs.......21 K5
Bishops Lydeard
  Somset.......12 C7
Bishop's Stortford
  Herts.......16 D5
Bishopsteignton
  Devon.......6 C4
Bishopston Swans.......19 J7
Bishopstone Swindn...13 M3
Bishop Sutton BaNES...13 G5
Bishop's Waltham
  Hants.......8 F4
Bitchfield Lincs.......30 F6
Bitton S Glos.......13 G4
Blaby Leics.......22 F1
Blackbrook Staffs.......28 E6
Blackburn Bl w D.......32 F4
Blackford P & K.......50 E6
Blackmill Brdgnd.......19 M7
Blackpool Bpool.......32 C3
Black Torrington
  Devon.......4 D6
Blackwater IoW.......8 F6
Blackwaterfoot
  N Ayrs.......44 C5
Blackwood Caerph.......12 C2
Blackwood S Lans.......45 L4
Bladon Oxon.......14 C3
Blaenau Ffestiniog
  Gwynd.......26 F5
Blaenavon Torfn.......12 D1
Blaengarw Brdgnd.......19 L6
Blaenporth Cerdgn...18 F2
Blagdon N Som.......12 F5
Blair Atholl P & K.......54 C7
Blairgowrie P & K.......51 G3
Blairmore Ag & B.......49 K5
Blakeney Gloucs.......13 G1
Blakesley Nhants.......23 G5
Blanchland Nthumb...43 G6
Blandford Forum
  Dorset.......7 L2
Blanefield Stirlg.......50 B8
Blaxton Donc.......34 D6
Blaydon Gatesd.......43 J5
Bleadney Somset.......12 F6
Bleadon N Som.......12 E5
Blean Kent.......11 J3
Bleddfa Powys.......20 F4
Bletchingley Surrey...10 B3
Bletchley M Keyn.......23 J6

Bletsoe Bed.......23 K4
Blewbury Oxon.......14 C5
Blickling Norfk.......25 J3
Blidworth Notts.......30 C4
Blindley Heath
  Surrey.......10 C4
Blisland Cnwll.......3 G4
Bloxham Oxon.......22 E6
Blubberhouses
  N York.......38 B7
Blue Anchor Somset...5 J3
Blyth Nthumb.......43 K4
Blyton Lincs.......34 E7
Boat of Garten
  Highld.......54 D3
Boddam Abers.......61 H5
Bodfari Denbgs.......27 J3
Bodfuan Gwynd.......26 C6
Bodiam E Susx.......10 F5
Bodmin Cnwll.......3 G4
Bognor Regis W Susx....9 J6
Bollington Ches E.......29 G3
Bolney W Susx.......10 B6
Bolsover Derbys.......29 L3
Bolton Bolton.......32 F6
Bolton Abbey N York...33 J2
Bolton le Sands
  Lancs.......37 H6
Bolventor Cnwll.......3 H3
Bonar Bridge Highld...64 C8
Bonchester Bridge
  Border.......42 D1
Bo'ness Falk.......46 A2
Bonnyrigg Mdloth.......46 D4
Bontnewydd Gwynd...26 D4
Bonvilston V Glam.......12 B4
Boot Cumb.......36 E3
Bootle Cumb.......36 E4
Bootle Sefton.......32 C7
Bordeaux Guern.......6 b1
Boreham Street
  E Susx.......10 E6
Borehamwood Herts...15 J4
Boroughbridge
  N York.......38 D6
Borough Green Kent...10 E3
Borrowash Derbys.......29 L6
Borth Cerdgn.......20 A2
Borth-y-Gest Gwynd...26 E6
Boscastle Cnwll.......3 G2
Bosham W Susx.......9 H5
Bosherston Pembks...18 D6
Boston Lincs.......31 J5
Boston Spa Leeds.......34 B3
Botesdale Suffk.......25 H7
Bothel Cumb.......41 M7
Bottesford Leics.......30 E6
Bough Beech Kent.......10 D4
Boughton Street
  Kent.......11 H3
Boulmer Nthumb.......47 M7
Bourne Lincs.......31 G7
Bournemouth
  Bmouth.......8 B6
Bourton Shrops.......21 K2
Bourton-on-the-
  Water Gloucs.......22 C7
Bovey Tracey Devon....6 B4
Bowes Dur.......37 M3
Bowmore Ag & B.......48 C7
Bowness-on-Solway
  Cumb.......41 M5
Box Wilts.......13 J4
Boxford Suffk.......17 H4
Bozeat Nhants.......23 J4
Bracadale Highld.......56 D5
Brackley Nhants.......23 G6
Bracknell Br For.......14 F6
Bradford C Brad.......33 K4
Bradford-on-Avon
  Wilts.......13 J5
Brading IoW.......8 F6
Bradwell Derbys.......29 J2
Bradwell-on-Sea
  Essex.......17 H6
Bradworthy Devon.......4 C6
Brae Shet.......61 b4
Braemar Abers.......54 E5
Braeswick Ork.......65 d2
Braidwood S Lans.......45 L3
Brailsford Derbys.......29 J5
Braintree Essex.......16 F5
Braithwaite Cumb.......36 F2
Bramdean Hants.......8 F3
Bramfield Suffk.......25 K7
Bramham Leeds.......34 B3
Bramhope Leeds.......33 L3
Bramley Hants.......14 D7
Bramley Surrey.......9 K2
Brampton Cambs.......23 M3
Brampton Cumb.......42 D5

Bramshaw Hants.......8 D4
Brancaster Norfk.......24 E2
Brandesburton
  E R Yk.......35 H3
Brandon Dur.......43 J7
Brandon Suffk.......24 E6
Brandon Warwks.......22 E3
Branscombe Devon.......6 E3
Bransgore Hants.......8 C6
Branston Lincs.......30 F3
Branthwaite Cumb.......36 D2
Brassington Derbys...29 J4
Brasted Kent.......10 D3
Bratton Wilts.......13 J6
Bratton Clovelly
  Devon.......3 K2
Bratton Fleming
  Devon.......4 F4
Braughing Herts.......16 C5
Braunton Devon.......4 D4
Brayford Devon.......4 F4
Breascleit W Isls.......62 g3
Breasclete W Isls.......62 g3
Brechfa Carmth.......19 H4
Brechin Angus.......55 J7
Brecon Powys.......20 E7
Brede E Susx.......11 G6
Bredenbury Herefs...21 K5
Bredhurst Kent.......10 F3
Bredon Worcs.......22 A6
Bredwardine Herefs...21 G6
Brendon Devon.......5 G3
Brent Knoll Somset...12 E6
Brentwood Essex.......16 E7
Brenzett Kent.......11 H5
Brereton Green
  Ches E.......28 E4
Brewood Staffs.......28 F8
Bride IoM.......36 C1
Bridestowe Devon.......3 L2
Bridge Kent.......11 J3
Bridgend Ag & B.......44 C4
Bridgend Ag & B.......48 C6
Bridgend Brdgnd.......19 L7
Bridge of Allan Stirlg...50 D6
Bridge of Cally P & K...51 G2
Bridge of Earn P & K...51 G5
Bridge of Orchy
  Ag & B.......53 K6
Bridge of Weir Rens...49 M6
Bridgnorth Shrops.......21 L2
Bridgwater Somset.......12 D7
Bridlington E R Yk.......39 L6
Bridport Dorset.......7 H3
Brierfield Lancs.......33 H3
Brigg N Linc.......35 G6
Brigham Cumb.......41 L8
Brighouse Calder.......33 K4
Brighstone IoW.......8 E7
Brightlingsea Essex...17 J5
Brighton Br & H.......10 B7
Brigstock Nhants.......23 K2
Brinklow Warwks.......22 E3
Brinkworth Wilts.......13 K3
Brinyan Ork.......65 c3
Bristol Bristl.......13 G4
Brixham Torbay.......6 C6
Brixton Devon.......3 L5
Brixworth Nhants.......23 H3
Broad Blunsdon
  Swindn.......13 L3
Broad Chalke Wilts...13 K8
Broadclyst Devon.......6 D3
Broadford Highld.......56 F6
Broad Haven Pembks...18 C5
Broadstairs Kent.......11 L3
Broadway Worcs.......22 C6
Broadwindsor
  Dorset.......7 G2
Brockdish Norfk.......25 J7
Brockenhurst Hants...8 D5
Brockford Street
  Suffk.......17 J3
Brockworth Gloucs...21 M8
Brodick N Ayrs.......44 D3
Brome Suffk.......25 H7
Bromfield Shrops.......21 J3
Bromham Bed.......23 K5
Bromley Gt Lon.......10 C2
Brompton-by-
  Sawdon N York...39 J5
Brompton Regis
  Somset.......5 H4
Bromsgrove Worcs...22 A3
Bromyard Herefs.......21 K5
Bronllys Powys.......20 F6
Brooke Norfk.......25 J5
Brookland Kent.......11 H5
Brookmans Park
  Herts.......15 J4
Broomhill Nthumb.......43 K2

Brora Highld.......64 F7
Broseley Shrops.......21 K1
Brotherton N York.......34 B4
Brotton R & Cl.......39 G2
Brough Cumb.......37 K2
Broughton Border.......46 B6
Broughton N Linc.......34 F6
Broughton-in-
  Furness Cumb.......36 F5
Broughton Poggs
  Oxon.......13 M2
Brownhills Wsall.......29 H8
Broxburn W Loth.......46 B3
Broxted Essex.......16 D5
Brundall Norfk.......25 K5
Bruton Somset.......13 G7
Brynamman Carmth...19 K5
Bryncrug Gwynd.......20 A1
Brynmawr Blae G.......12 C1
Bubwith E R Yk.......34 D3
Buchlyvie Stirlg.......50 B7
Buckden Cambs.......23 M4
Buckden N York.......37 M5
Buckfastleigh Devon....6 B5
Buckhaven Fife.......51 H6
Buckhorn Weston
  Dorset.......13 H8
Buckie Moray.......60 B3
Buckingham Bucks...23 G6
Buckland Herts.......16 C4
Bucklers Hard Hants....8 E5
Buckley Flints.......27 L4
Bucklow Hill Ches E...28 E2
Buckminster Leics.......30 E7
Bude Cnwll.......4 B6
Budleigh Salterton
  Devon.......6 D4
Bugle Cnwll.......2 F5
Builth Wells Powys...20 E5
Bulford Wilts.......8 C2
Bulkington Warwks...22 E2
Bulwick Nhants.......23 K2
Bunessan Ag & B.......48 C2
Bungay Suffk.......25 K6
Bunny Notts.......30 C6
Buntingford Herts.......16 C4
Bunwell Norfk.......25 H6
Burbage Wilts.......13 M5
Bures Essex.......17 G4
Burford Oxon.......13 M1
Burgess Hill W Susx...10 B6
Burgh by Sands
  Cumb.......42 B6
Burgh Castle Norfk...25 L5
Burghead Moray.......59 J3
Burghfield W Berk.......14 D6
Burgh le Marsh Lincs...31 K4
Burley Hants.......8 C5
Burleydam Ches E.......28 D5
Burley in
  Wharfedale
  C Brad.......33 K3
Burlton Shrops.......28 C7
Burneston N York.......38 C5
Burnham Market
  Norfk.......24 F2
Burnham-on-Crouch
  Essex.......17 H7
Burnham-on-Sea
  Somset.......12 D6
Burnham Overy
  Staithe Norfk.......24 F2
Burnley Lancs.......33 G4
Burnopfield Dur.......43 J6
Burntisland Fife.......46 C2
Burravoe Shet.......61 d3
Burrelton P & K.......51 G3
Burrington Devon.......4 F5
Burry Port Carmth.......19 H6
Burscough Bridge
  Lancs.......32 D5
Bursledon Hants.......8 E5
Burton Ches E.......27 L3
Burton Agnes E R Yk...39 K6
Burton Bradstock
  Dorset.......7 H3
Burton Fleming
  E R Yk.......39 K6
Burton-in-Kendal
  Cumb.......37 H5
Burton Joyce Notts...30 C5
Burton Latimer
  Nhants.......23 J3
Burton upon
  Stather N Linc.......34 F5
Burton upon Trent
  Staffs.......29 J7
Burwash E Susx.......10 E5
Burwell Cambs.......16 E1
Burwick Ork.......65 c6

Bury Bury 33 G5
Bury St Edmunds Suffk 17 G2
Bushey Herts 15 H4
Butley Suffk 17 L3
Buttermere Cumb 36 E2
Butterwick Lincs 31 J5
Buttington Powys 27 K8
Buxted E Susx 10 D6
Buxton Derbys 29 H3
Bwlch Powys 20 F7
Byfleet Surrey 15 H7
Bylchau Conwy 27 H4
Byrness Nthumb 42 F2

C

Cadgwith Cnwll 2 D8
Caerleon Newpt 12 E3
Caernarfon Gwynd 26 D4
Caerphilly Caerph 12 C3
Caersws Powys 20 E2
Caerwent Mons 12 F3
Caerwys Flints 27 J3
Cairndow Ag & B 49 K3
Cairnryan D & G 40 B5
Caister-on-Sea Norfk 25 L5
Caistor Lincs 35 H6
Caldbeck Cumb 42 B7
Caldecott Rutlnd 23 J2
Calder Bridge Cumb 36 D2
Caldercruix N Lans 45 L2
Caldicot Mons 12 F3
Calfsound Ork 65 d2
Calgary Ag & B 52 B5
Callander Stirlg 50 B6
Callington Cnwll 3 J4
Calne Wilts 13 K4
Calshot Hants 8 E5
Calvine P & K 54 C7
Camber E Susx 11 H6
Camberley Surrey 14 F7
Cambo Nthumb 43 H4
Camborne Cnwll 2 C6
Cambourne Cambs 16 B2
Cambridge Cambs 16 C2
Cambridge Gloucs 13 H2
Cambuslang S Lans 45 K2
Camden Town Gt Lon 15 K5
Camelford Cnwll 3 G3
Campbeltown Ag & B 44 B8
Candlesby Lincs 31 K3
Cannich Highld 58 C6
Cannington Somset 12 D7
Cannock Staffs 29 G8
Canonbie D & G 42 C4
Canterbury Kent 11 J3
Canvey Island Essex 16 F8
Caoles Ag & B 48 b2
Capel Surrey 9 L2
Capel Bangor Cerdgn .. 20 B3
Capel Curig Conwy 26 F4
Capel St Mary Suffk .. 17 J4
Caputh P & K 50 F3
Carbost Highld 56 D6
Cardiff Cardif 12 C4
Cardigan Cerdgn 18 E2
Cardington Bed 23 L5
Cardross Ag & B 49 L5
Carew Pembks 18 D6
Carfraemill Border 46 F4
Carhampton Somset ... 5 J3
Cark Cumb 37 G5
Carlabhagh W Isls 62 g3
Carlisle Cumb 42 C6
Carlops Border 46 C4
Carloway W Isls 62 g3
Carlton N York 34 D4
Carlton N York 38 A5
Carlton-on-Trent Notts 30 E4
Carluke S Lans 45 L3
Carmarthen Carmth ... 19 G4
Carnaby E R Yk 39 K6
Carnforth Lancs 37 H6
Carno Powys 20 D2
Carnon Downs Cnwll 2 D6
Carnoustie Angus 51 K4
Carnwath S Lans 46 A5
Carradale Ag & B 44 C4
Carrbridge Highld 59 H6
Carrefour Jersey 7 b1
Carrick Castle Ag & B.. 49 K6
Carronbridge D & G 41 J3
Carrutherstown D & G 41 L5
Carsphairn D & G 40 F3
Carstairs S Lans 45 M3
Carterton Oxon 14 A3

Cartmel Cumb 37 G5
Castel Guern 6 a2
Casterton Cumb 37 J5
Castle Acre Norfk 24 F4
Castlebay W Isls 62 b14
Castle Carrock Cumb .. 42 D6
Castle Cary Somset 13 G7
Castle Donington Leics 29 L6
Castle Douglas D & G .. 41 H5
Castleford Wakefd 34 B4
Castle Hedingham Essex 16 F4
Castlemartin Pembks .. 18 C6
Castle Rising Norfk 24 D4
Castleside Dur 43 H6
Castleton Derbys 29 H2
Castleton N York 39 G3
Castleton Newpt 12 D3
Castletown Highld 65 H2
Castletown IoM 36 b4
Caterham Surrey 10 C3
Catfield Norfk 25 K4
Caton Lancs 37 H6
Catrine E Ayrs 45 J5
Catsfield E Susx 10 F6
Catterick N York 38 C4
Caunton Notts 30 D4
Cawdor Highld 59 G4
Cawsand Cnwll 3 K5
Caxton Cambs 16 B2
Caythorpe Lincs 30 F5
Cayton N York 39 K5
Cemaes IoA 26 C1
Cemmaes Road Powys 20 C1
Ceres Fife 51 J5
Cerne Abbas Dorset .. 7 J2
Cerrigydrudion Conwy 27 H5
Chadderton Oldham ... 33 H6
Chadlington Oxon 14 B2
Chagford Devon 6 A3
Chale IoW 8 E7
Chalfont St Giles Bucks 15 G4
Chalfont St Peter Bucks 15 G5
Chalford Gloucs 13 J2
Challacombe Devon .. 4 F3
Challock Kent 11 H3
Chandler's Ford Hants 8 E4
Chapel-en-le-Frith Derbys 29 H2
Chapel St Leonards Lincs 31 L3
Chapeltown Sheff 34 A6
Chapmanslade Wilts ... 13 J6
Chard Somset 6 F2
Charing Kent 11 H4
Charlbury Oxon 14 B2
Charlecote Warwks ... 22 D5
Charlton Kings Gloucs 22 A7
Charlton Marshall Dorset 7 L2
Charlwood Surrey 10 B4
Charmouth Dorset 7 G3
Chartham Kent 11 J3
Chatburn Lancs 33 G3
Chatham Medway 10 F2
Chatteris Cambs 24 B7
Chatton Nthumb 47 K6
Chawleigh Devon 4 H4
Chawton Hants 9 G3
Cheadle Staffs 29 G5
Cheadle Stockp 33 H7
Cheddar Somset 12 F6
Cheddleton Staffs 29 G5
Chelford Ches E 28 F3
Chelmsford Essex 16 F6
Cheltenham Gloucs 22 A7
Chepstow Mons 12 F3
Cheriton Hants 8 F3
Cheriton Fitzpaine Devon 6 A1
Chertsey Surrey 15 G6
Chesham Bucks 15 G6
Cheshunt Herts 15 K4
Chester Ches W 28 B3
Chesterfield Derbys 29 K3
Chester-le-Street Dur.. 43 K5
Chew Magna BaNES 13 G5
Chewton Mendip Somset 13 G6
Chicheley M Keyn 23 J5
Chichester W Susx 9 H5
Chickerell Dorset 7 J4
Chicklade Wilts 13 J7
Chiddingfold Surrey .. 9 J3

Chieveley W Berk 14 C6
Chigwell Essex 16 C7
Childer Thornton Ches W 28 B3
Chilham Kent 11 J3
Chillington Devon 6 B7
Chilmark Wilts 13 K7
Chilsworthy Devon .. 4 C6
Chilton Foliat Wilts 14 A6
Chineham Hants 14 D7
Chinnor Oxon 14 E4
Chippenham Cambs .. 16 E1
Chippenham Wilts 13 J4
Chipperfield Herts 15 G4
Chipping Lancs 32 F3
Chipping Campden Gloucs 22 C6
Chipping Norton Oxon 22 D7
Chipping Ongar Essex 16 D6
Chipping Sodbury S Glos 13 H3
Chipping Warden Nhants 22 F5
Chirbury Shrops 21 G1
Chirk Wrexhm 27 L6
Chirnside Border 47 J4
Chiseldon Swindn 13 M4
Chitterne Wilts 13 K6
Chittlehamholt Devon 4 F5
Chobham Surrey 15 G7
Cholderton Wilts 8 C2
Chorley Lancs 32 E5
Chorleywood Herts 15 G4
Christchurch Dorset .. 8 C6
Chudleigh Devon 6 C4
Chudleigh Knighton Devon 6 C4
Chulmleigh Devon .. 4 F6
Churchill Oxon 14 A2
Churchstoke Powys 21 G2
Church Stretton Shrops 21 H2
Churston Ferrers Torbay 6 C6
Churt Surrey 9 H3
Cinderford Gloucs 21 K8
Cirencester Gloucs 13 K2
Clachan Ag & B 44 B3
Clachan Highld 56 E5
Clackmannan Clacks.. 50 E7
Clacton-on-Sea Essex.. 17 J5
Clanfield Oxon 14 A4
Claonaig Ag & B 44 C3
Clapham Bed 23 K5
Clapham N York 37 K6
Clare Suffk 16 F3
Clatt Abers 60 C6
Claverdon Warwks 22 C4
Clavering Essex 16 D4
Clawton Devon 4 C7
Clay Cross Derbys 29 K4
Claydon Suffk 17 J3
Cleator Moor Cumb 36 D2
Cleethorpes NE Lin ... 35 J6
Cleeve N Som 12 F5
Cleeve Hill Gloucs 22 B7
Cleobury Mortimer Shrops 21 K3
Cleobury North Shrops 21 K2
Clevedon N Som 12 E4
Cleveleys Lancs 32 C3
Cley next the Sea Norfk 25 G2
Cliffe Medway 10 F2
Cliffe N York 34 D4
Cliffe Woods Medway .. 10 F2
Clifton Cumb 37 H2
Clifton upon Teme Worcs 21 L4
Climping W Susx 9 K5
Clitheroe Lancs 33 G3
Clola Abers 61 G5
Clophill C Beds 23 L6
Closworth Somset 7 H2
Cloughton N York 39 J4
Clova Angus 55 G6
Clovelly Devon 4 C5
Clovenfords Border .. 46 E6
Clowne Derbys 30 B3
Clows Top Worcs 21 L3
Clun Shrops 21 G3
Clydach Swans 19 J6
Clydebank W Duns 45 H2
Clynder Ag & B 49 K5
Clynnog-fawr Gwynd .. 26 D5
Clyro Powys 20 F6
Clyst St Mary Devon .. 6 D3

Coalport Wrekin 21 K1
Coalville Leics 29 L7
Coatbridge N Lans ... 45 K2
Cobham Kent 10 E2
Cockburnspath Border 47 H3
Cockermouth Cumb 41 L8
Cocking W Susx 9 J4
Coddenham Suffk 17 J2
Codford St Mary Wilts 13 K7
Codicote Herts 15 J3
Codnor Derbys 29 L5
Codsall Staffs 21 M1
Coedpoeth Wrexhm ... 27 L5
Coggeshall Essex 17 G5
Colchester Essex 17 H5
Cold Ash W Berk 14 C6
Cold Ashby Nhants 23 G3
Cold Ashton S Glos 13 H4
Coldingham Border 47 J3
Cold Norton Essex 17 G7
Coldstream Border 47 H5
Coleford Gloucs 13 G1
Colerne Wilts 13 J4
Coleshill Warwks 22 C2
Colintraive Ag & B 49 J6
Collier's End Herts 15 K2
Collieston Abers 61 G6
Collingbourne Ducis Wilts 13 M6
Collingham Leeds 34 B3
Colmonell S Ayrs 40 C3
Colne Lancs 33 H3
Colne Engaine Essex.. 17 G4
Coln St Aldwyns Gloucs 13 L2
Colpy Abers 60 D6
Colsterworth Lincs 30 F7
Coltishall Norfk 25 J4
Colwell Nthumb 43 G4
Colwyn Bay Conwy 27 G2
Colyford Devon 6 F3
Colyton Devon 6 F3
Combe Martin Devon .. 4 E2
Compton Surrey 9 J2
Compton W Berk 14 C5
Comrie P & K 50 D5
Congleton Ches E 28 F4
Congresbury N Som .. 12 E5
Coningsby Lincs 31 H4
Conington Cambs 23 M2
Conisbrough Donc 34 C6
Coniston Cumb 36 F4
Connah's Quay Flints .. 27 L3
Connel Ag & B 52 F7
Conon Bridge Highld .. 58 E4
Consett Dur 43 H6
Constantine Cnwll 2 D7
Contin Highld 58 D4
Conwy Conwy 27 G3
Cookham W & M 14 F5
Coolham W Susx 9 L4
Coombe Bissett Wilts.. 8 B3
Coombe Hill Gloucs 21 M7
Copdock Suffk 17 J3
Copford Green Essex.. 17 G5
Copley Dur 38 B2
Copplestone Devon .. 5 G6
Copthorne W Susx 10 B4
Corbiere Jersey 7 a2
Corbridge Nthumb 43 G5
Corby Nhants 23 J2
Corby Glen Lincs 30 F7
Corfe Somset 6 F1
Corfe Castle Dorset 7 M4
Corgarff Abers 55 G4
Cornhill-on-Tweed Nthumb 47 H5
Cornwood Devon 3 L5
Corpach Highld 53 H3
Corrie N Ayrs 44 D4
Corris Gwynd 26 F8
Corsham Wilts 13 J4
Corston Wilts 13 J3
Corton Suffk 25 M6
Corwen Denbgs 27 J5
Coryton Thurr 16 F8
Cosby Leics 22 F2
Cotebrook Ches W 28 D4
Cotherstone Dur 38 A2
Cottenham Cambs 16 C1
Cottered Herts 16 B4
Cottingham E R Yk 35 G4
Coulport Ag & B 49 K5
Coulter S Lans 46 B6
Countesthorpe Leics.. 23 G2
Coupar Angus P & K .. 51 G3
Cove Highld 62 D8
Coventry Covtry 22 E3
Coverack Cnwll 2 D8

Cowbit Lincs............31 H7
Cowbridge V Glam 12 B4
Cowden Kent.............10 D4
Cowdenbeath Fife.....51 G7
Cowes IoW 8 E6
Cowfold W Susx..........9 L4
Cowling N York..........33 J3
Coxheath Kent..........10 F5
Coxwold N York.........38 E5
Coylton S Ayrs..........45 H6
Coylumbridge Highld ..54 D3
Crackington Haven
Cnwll.....................4 B7
Cracoe N York 37 M7
Crafthole Cnwll............3 J5
Craigellachie Moray ..59 L5
Craighouse Ag & B.....48 D6
Craignure Ag & B.......52 E6
Craigrothie Fife.........51 J5
Crail Fife 51 L6
Crailing Border 47 G7
Cramlington Nthumb...43 K4
Cranborne Dorset........8 B4
Cranbrook Kent..........10 F5
Cranfield C Beds........23 K6
Cranham Gloucs.........21 M8
Cranleigh Surrey.........9 K2
Cranshaws Border 47 G4
Crarae Ag & B............49 H4
Craster Nthumb.........47 M7
Crathie Abers 54 F5
Crathorne N York 38 E3
Craven Arms Shrops ...21 H3
Crawford S Lans.........46 A7
Crawfordjohn S Lans...45 M5
Crawley W Susx..........10 B5
Crawley Down
W Susx 10 B4
Creag Ghoraidh
W Isls 62 c10
Creagorry W Isls 62 c10
Credenhill Herefs 21 H6
Crediton Devon...........5 G7
Creetown D & G.........40 F6
Cregneash IoM 36 a4
Cressage Shrops.........21 K1
Crewe Ches E 28 E4
Crewkerne Somset.......7 G2
Crianlarich Stirlg........53 K7
Criccieth Gwynd 26 D6
Crickhowell Powys......20 F7
Cricklade Wilts 13 L3
Crieff P & K 50 D5
Crimond Abers...........61 H4
Crinan Ag & B............49 G4
Cringleford Norfk.......25 J5
Crockernwell Devon......6 B3
Crocketford D & G......41 J4
Croglin Cumb............42 D6
Cromarty Highld.........59 G3
Cromdale Highld 59 J6
Cromer Norfk............25 J2
Cromford Derbys........29 K4
Cromwell Notts..........30 E4
Crook Dur..................43 J7
Crooklands Cumb.......37 H5
Cropredy Oxon 22 F5
Cropton N York 39 G4
Crosby IoM 36 b3
Crosby Sefton............32 C6
Crossford Fife............46 B2
Crossford S Lans........45 L3
Cross Hands Carmth ...19 H5
Crosshill S Ayrs.........45 G6
Cross in Hand E Susx ..10 D6
Crosskeys Caerph........12 D3
Crossmichael D & G....41 H5
Crossway Green
Worcs....................21 M4
Crosthwaite Cumb.....37 G4
Crowborough E Susx...10 D5
Crowcombe Somset.....5 K4
Crowhurst E Susx......10 F6
Crowland Lincs..........31 H8
Crowle N Linc............34 E5
Crowthorne Wokham ..14 F7
Croxton Kerrial Leics ..30 E6
Croy Highld...............59 G4
Croyde Devon..............4 D4
Croydon Gt Lon 15 K7
Cruden Bay Abers 61 H5
Crudgington Wrekin ...28 D7
Crudwell Wilts............13 K3
Crynant Neath...........19 K5
Cuckfield W Susx.......10 B5
Cuckney Notts...........30 C3
Cuddington Ches W....28 B7
Cudworth Barns.........34 B6
Cuffley Herts..............15 K4
Culgaith Cumb...........37 J1
Cullen Moray.............60 C3

Cullompton Devon.......5 J6
Culmstock Devon.........5 K6
Cumbernauld N Lans...45 L1
Cuminestown Abers....60 E4
Cummertrees D & G....41 L5
Cumnock E Ayrs........45 J5
Cumnor Oxon 14 C4
Cumrew Cumb............42 D6
Cupar Fife 51 J5
Curry Rivel Somset....12 E8
Cwmbran Torfn..........12 D2
Cwmystwyth Cerdgn ...20 C3
Cymer Neath.............19 L6
Cynwyl Elfed Carmth ..19 G4

D

Dailly S Ayrs.............40 D2
Dairsie Fife...............51 J5
Dalbeattie D & G.......41 J5
Dalby IoM 36 a3
Dale Pembks.............18 B5
Dalgety Bay Fife 46 C2
Dalhalvaig Highld.......64 E3
Dalkeith Mdloth.........46 D3
Dallas Moray.............59 J4
Dalmally Ag & B.........53 J7
Dalmellington E Ayrs...45 H7
Dalry N Ayrs.............45 G3
Dalrymple E Ayrs.......45 G6
Dalston Cumb............42 B6
Dalton D & G............41 L4
Dalton-in-Furness
Cumb....................36 F6
Dalwhinnie Highld 54 A5
Damerham Hants.........8 B4
Danbury Essex...........16 F6
Darlington Darltn.......38 C2
Darras Hall Nthumb....43 J5
Darrington Wakefd 34 B5
Dartford Kent............10 D2
Dartington Devon........6 B5
Dartmouth Devon........6 C6
Darvel E Ayrs............45 J4
Darwen Bl w D 32 F5
Datchet W & M 15 G6
Dava Highld..............59 H5
Davenham Ches W......28 D3
Daventry Nhants........23 G4
Daviot Highld............58 F5
Dawlish Devon............6 C4
Deal Kent 11 L3
Dearham Cumb..........41 L7
Debenham Suffk........17 J2
Deddington Oxon 22 F6
Dedham Essex...........17 H4
Deeping St James
Lincs....................31 H8
Deeping St Nicholas
Lincs....................31 H7
Deganwy Conwy.........27 G2
Delabole Cnwll............3 G3
Denbigh Denbgs........27 J3
Denby Dale Kirk.........33 L6
Denham Bucks...........15 G5
Denholm Border.........46 F7
Denmead Hants...........9 G5
Dennington Suffk.......17 K1
Denny Falk................50 D8
Densole Kent.............11 K4
Dent Cumb................37 K5
Denton Tamesd.........33 H7
Derby C Derb............29 K6
Derbyhaven IoM 36 b4
Dereham Norfk..........25 G4
Dersingham Norfk......24 E3
Dervaig Ag & B..........52 B5
Desborough Nhants ...23 H3
Desford Leics............22 F1
Devil's Bridge Cerdgn..20 B3
Devizes Wilts............13 K5
Dewsbury Kirk...........33 L5
Dial Post W Susx.........9 L4
Didcot Oxon 14 C5
Didmarton Gloucs......13 J4
Digby Lincs...............31 G4
Dilwyn Herefs...........21 H5
Dinas-Mawddwy
Gwynd..................27 G7
Dingwall Highld.........58 E4
Dinnington Rothm......30 B2
Dippen Ag & B...........44 C4
Diseworth Leics.........29 L1
Dishforth N York 38 D6
Disley Ches E............29 G2
Diss Norfk................25 H7
Ditchling E Susx........10 B6
Dittisham Devon..........6 C6
Ditton Priors Shrops ...21 K2

Dobwalls Cnwll............3 H4
Docking Norfk...........24 E3
Doddington Cambs.....24 B6
Doddington Kent........11 G3
Doddington
Nthumb.................47 K6
Dodworth Barns........33 L6
Dolgellau Gwynd 26 F7
Dollar Clacks............50 E6
Dolphinton S Lans.....46 B5
Dolton Devon..............4 E6
Dolwyddelan Conwy ...26 F5
Doncaster Donc.........34 C6
Donington Lincs.........31 H6
Dorchester Dorset.......7 K3
Dorchester Oxon.......14 D4
Dordon Warwks.........22 D1
Dores Highld.............58 E5
Dorking Surrey...........9 L2
Dornie Highld............57 H6
Dornoch Highld.........59 G1
Dorrington Shrops.....21 J1
Dorstone Herefs........21 G6
Douglas IoM 36 c3
Douglas S Lans..........45 L5
Dounby Ork...............65 b3
Doune Stirlg.............50 C6
Dousland Devon..........3 L4
Dover Kent...............11 L4
Doveridge Derbys.......29 H6
Dowally P & K............50 E3
Downderry Cnwll.........3 J5
Downham Market
Norfk....................24 D5
Downton Wilts............8 C4
Drakes Broughton
Worcs....................22 A5
Draycott Somset........12 F6
Drayton Norfk...........25 J4
Drayton Oxon 14 C4
Driffield E R Yk..........39 J7
Drimnin Highld..........52 C5
Droitwich Worcs........22 A4
Dronfield Derbys........29 K3
Droxford Hants..........8 F4
Drumbeg Highld.........63 G4
Drummore D & G.......40 C7
Drumnadrochit
Highld 58 D6
Drymen Stirlg...........50 A7
Drynoch Highld.........56 D6
Duddington Nhants....23 K1
Dudley Dudley 22 A2
Dufftown Moray........59 L5
Duffus Moray............59 K3
Dulnain Bridge
Highld 59 H6
Dulverton Somset.......5 H4
Dumbarton W Duns....49 M5
Dumfries D & G.........41 K4
Dunbar E Loth..........47 G2
Dunbeath Highld........65 H5
Dunblane Stirlg.........50 D6
Dunchurch Warwks....22 F3
Dundee C Dund.........51 J4
Dundonald S Ayrs......45 G4
Dundonnell Highld.....57 K1
Dundrennan D & G.....41 H6
Dunfermline Fife.......46 B2
Dunkeld P & K...........50 F3
Dunlop E Ayrs...........45 H3
Dunnet Highld...........65 H2
Dunning P & K...........50 F5
Dunoon Ag & B..........49 K5
Dunragit D & G..........40 C6
Duns Border.............47 H4
Dunscore D & G.........41 J4
Dunsfold Surrey..........9 K3
Dunsford Devon..........6 B3
Dunsop Bridge
Lancs....................32 F2
Dunstable C Beds......15 G2
Dunster Somset..........5 J3
Duntish Dorset...........7 K2
Dunure S Ayrs...........44 F6
Dunvant Swans.........19 J6
Dunvegan Highld........56 C4
Dunwich Suffk...........25 L4
Durham Dur..............43 K7
Durness Highld..........63 J2
Duror Highld.............53 G5
Durrington Wilts.........8 C2
Durris Abers..............55 L5
Dursley Gloucs..........13 H2
Duxford Cambs..........16 D3
Dyce C Aber.............55 M3
Dyffryn Ardudwy
Gwynd..................26 E7
Dymchurch Kent........11 J5
Dymock Gloucs..........21 K7

E

Eaglesfield D & G.......42 A4
Eaglesham E Rens.....45 J3
Ealing Gt Lon 15 J5
Earby Lancs..............33 H3
Eardisley Herefs........21 G5
Earith Cambs............24 B7
Earley Wokham..........14 E6
Earls Barton Nhants ...23 J4
Earls Colne Essex......17 G4
Earl Shilton Leics.......22 F1
Earlston Border.........46 F6
Earsham Norfk..........25 K6
Easdale Ag & B..........48 F2
Easebourne W Susx 9 J4
Easington Dur...........43 L7
Easington E R Yk.......35 K5
Easingwold N York.....38 E6
East Ayton N York 39 J3
East Barkwith Lincs....31 H2
East Bergholt Suffk 17 J4
Eastbourne E Susx.....10 E7
East Chinnock
Somset...................7 H1
Eastchurch Kent........11 H2
East Cowes IoW...........8 E6
East Dean E Susx......10 D8
East Dean W Susx.......9 J4
East Goscote Leics.....30 C7
East Grinstead
W Susx 10 C4
East Harling Norfk......25 G6
East Hoathly E Susx...10 D6
East Horsley Surrey....15 H8
East Ilsley W Berk......14 C5
East Kilbride S Lans....45 J3
East Knoyle Wilts.......13 J7
East Lavant W Susx.....9 H5
Eastleigh Hants..........8 E4
East Linton E Loth......46 F3
East Lulworth Dorset....7 L4
Easton Suffk.............17 K2
East Prawle Devon......6 B7
East Preston W Susx....9 K5
Eastriggs D & G.........42 A5
East Rudham Norfk.....24 F3
Eastry Kent..............11 L3
East Saltoun E Loth....46 E3
East Stoke Notts........30 D5
East Wittering
W Susx 9 H6
East Witton N York.....38 B5
Eastwood Notts.........29 L5
Eaton Socon Cambs....23 L4
Ebbw Vale Blae G......12 C1
Ebchester Dur...........43 H6
Ecclefechan D & G.....41 M4
Eccles Border............47 H5
Eccleshall Staffs.........28 F6
Echt Abers................55 K4
Eckington Derbys.......29 L2
Eckington Worcs........22 A6
Edderton Highld.........58 F2
Eddleston Border.......46 C5
Edenbridge Kent........10 C4
Edinbane Highld.........56 D4
Edinburgh C Edin 46 C3
Edlington Lincs..........31 H3
Edmundbyers Dur......43 H6
Ednam Border...........47 G6
Edwinstowe Notts......30 C3
Edzell Angus.............55 J7
Effingham Surrey.......15 H7
Eggesford Devon.........4 F6
Eggleston Dur...........37 M2
Egham Surrey...........15 G6
Eglingham Nthumb.....47 K7
Eglwyswrw Pembks....18 E3
Egremont Cumb.........36 D3
Egton Bridge N York...39 H3
Elan Village Powys.....20 D4
Elgin Moray...............59 K3
Elgol Highld..............56 E7
Elham Kent...............11 J4
Elie Fife 51 K6
Elkesley Notts...........30 D3
Elkstone Gloucs.........13 K1
Elland Calder............33 K5
Ellesmere Shrops.......28 B6
Ellesmere Port
Ches W..................28 B3
Ellingham Norfk.........25 K6
Ellon Abers...............61 G6
Elloughton E R Yk......34 F4
Elmstead Market
Essex....................17 H5
Elsdon Nthumb..........43 G3
Elsrickle S Lans.........46 B5
Elstead Surrey............9 J2

Elstree Herts 15 J4
Elterwater Cumb. 37 G3
Eltisley Cambs 16 B2
Elton Cambs 23 L2
Elveden Suffk. 24 F7
Elvetham Heath
 Hants 14 E7
Elvington C York. 34 D3
Elworthy Somset 5 J4
Ely Cambs 24 C7
Embleton Nthumb. 47 M7
Embo Highld. 64 E8
Empingham Rutlnd. 30 F8
Emsworth Hants 9 H5
Enderby Leics 22 F1
Enfield Gt Lon 15 K4
Ennerdale Bridge
 Cumb. 36 D2
Enstone Oxon 14 B2
Epping Essex 16 C6
Epsom Surrey 15 J7
Epworth N Linc. 34 E6
Errogie Highld. 58 E6
Errol P & K. 51 H4
Erwood Powys 20 E6
Esher Surrey 15 H7
Eskdale Green Cumb. 36 E4
Eskdalemuir D & G. 42 A3
Essendine Rutlnd. 31 G8
Essendon Herts 15 J3
Eston R & Cl. 38 E2
Etal Nthumb. 47 J6
Etchingham E Susx. 10 F5
Eton W & M 15 G6
Ettington Warwks 22 D5
Ettrick Border 46 D7
Ettrickbridge Border 46 E7
Evanton Highld. 58 E3
Evercreech Somset. 13 G7
Eversley Hants 14 E7
Evesham Worcs 22 B6
Ewen Gloucs. 15 K2
Ewhurst Surrey. 9 K2
Ewyas Harold Herefs 21 H7
Exbridge Somset. 5 H5
Exeter Devon 6 C3
Exford Somset. 5 H4
Exminster Devon 6 C3
Exmouth Devon 6 D4
Eye C Pete 23 M1
Eye Suffk. 25 H7
Eyemouth Border 47 J4
Eynsford Kent 10 D2
Eynsham Oxon 14 B3

F

Failsworth Oldham 33 H6
Fairbourne Gwynd. 26 E8
Fairford Gloucs. 13 L2
Fairlie N Ayrs 44 F3
Fairlight E Susx. 11 G6
Fakenham Norfk. 24 F3
Fala Mdloth 46 E4
Faldingworth Lincs. 31 G2
Falfield S Glos 13 G3
Falkirk Falk 50 E8
Falkland Fife 51 H6
Falmouth Cnwll 2 E7
Falstone Nthumb. 42 E3
Fareham Hants 8 F5
Faringdon Oxon 14 A4
Farnborough Hants 14 F7
Farnell Angus 51 L2
Farnham Surrey 9 H2
Farnham Common
 Bucks 15 G5
Farningham Kent 10 D2
Far Sawrey Cumb. 37 G4
Fauldhouse W Loth. 45 M2
Faversham Kent 11 H3
Fawley Hants 8 E5
Fazeley Staffs 22 C1
Fearnan P & K. 50 C3
Fearnhead Suffk. 17 K4
Felsted Essex 16 E5
Felton Nthumb. 43 J2
Feltwell Norfk. 24 E6
Fenny Bentley
 Derbys 29 J5
Fenny Bridges Devon... 6 E3
Fenny Compton
 Warwks 22 E5
Fenny Drayton Leics 22 E1
Fenwick N Ayrs 45 H4
Ferndown Dorset. 8 B5
Fernhill Heath Worcs. 21 M4
Fernhurst W Susx. 9 J3
Fernilee Derbys 29 G3

Ferring W Susx. 9 K5
Ferryhill Dur. 43 K8
Fettercairn Abers. 55 K6
Ffestiniog Gwynd. 26 F5
Filby Norfk 25 L4
Filey N York 39 K5
Fincham Norfk 24 E5
Finchingfield Essex. 16 E4
Findhorn Moray 59 J3
Findochty Moray 60 C3
Findon W Susx. 9 L5
Finedon Nhants. 23 J3
Finningham Suffk. 17 H1
Finningley Donc. 34 D6
Finstown Ork. 65 b4
Fintry Stirlg. 50 B7
Fionnphort Ag & B. 48 C2
Firle E Susx. 10 D7
Fishbourne IoW 8 F6
Fishguard Pembks. 18 C3
Fittleworth W Susx. 9 K4
Fitzhead Somset. 5 K4
Five Oaks Jersey 7 c2
Fladdabister Shet 61 c6
Flamborough E R Yk 39 L6
Flamstead Herts. 15 H3
Fleet Hants 14 F7
Fleetwood Lancs. 32 C3
Flimby Cumb 41 K7
Flint Flints. 27 K3
Flitwick C Beds 23 K6
Flixton N York 39 K5
Flore Nhants 23 G4
Fochabers Moray 59 L4
Folkestone Kent. 11 K5
Folkingham Lincs. 31 G6
Fontmell Magna
 Dorset. 7 L1
Fontwell W Susx. 9 J5
Ford Nthumb. 47 J6
Fordcombe Kent. 10 D4
Fordingbridge Hants. 8 C4
Fordoun Abers. 55 K6
Fordwich Kent. 11 J3
Forest Guern. 6 a2
Forest Row E Susx. 10 C5
Forfar Angus. 51 J2
Formby Sefton 32 C6
Forres Moray 59 J4
Fort Augustus Highld. 58 C7
Fortevoit P & K. 50 F5
Forth S Lans 45 M3
Fortingall P & K. 50 C3
Forton Lancs. 32 E2
Fortrose Highld. 58 F4
Fortuneswell Dorset. 7 J4
Fort William Highld. 53 H4
Foston Lincs. 30 E5
Four Crosses Powys. 27 L7
Four Marks Hants. 9 G3
Fowey Cnwll 3 G5
Fownhope Herefs. 21 J6
Foxdale IoM 36 b3
Foyers Highld. 58 D7
Framlingham Suffk. 17 K2
Frampton Dorset. 7 J3
Frant E Susx. 10 E5
Fraserburgh Abers. 61 G3
Freckenham Suffk. 24 D8
Freckleton Lancs. 32 D4
Frensham Surrey. 9 H2
Freshwater IoW 8 D6
Fressingfield Suffk. 25 J7
Freswick Highld. 65 J2
Fridaythorpe E R Yk 39 H7
Frilford Oxon 14 B4
Frinton-on-Sea Essex... 17 K5
Friockheim Angus. 51 K2
Fritton Norfk 25 L5
Frizington Cumb. 36 D2
Frocester Gloucs. 13 H2
Frodsham Ches W. 28 C3
Frome Somset. 13 H6
Froxfield Wilts. 14 A6
Funtington W Susx. 9 H5
Furnace Ag & B. 49 J4
Furness Vale Derbys 29 G2
Fyfield Essex 16 D6
Fyfield Oxon 14 B4
Fyvie Abers. 60 E5

G

Gailey Staffs 28 F8
Gainford Dur. 38 B2
Gainsborough Lincs. 34 E7
Gairloch Highld. 57 H2
Gairlochy Highld. 53 J3
Galashiels Border 46 E6

Galgate Lancs. 37 H7
Galston E Ayrs. 45 I14
Gamlingay Cambs. 16 B3
Gamston Notts. 30 D3
Ganllwyd Gwynd 26 F7
Garboldisham Norfk. 25 G7
Gardenstown Abers. 60 E3
Garelochhead Ag & B. 49 K4
Garforth Leeds 34 B4
Gargrave N York 33 H2
Garlieston D & G. 40 F6
Garlogie Abers. 55 L4
Garrigill Cumb. 42 E7
Garstang Lancs. 32 E3
Garth Powys. 20 D5
Garvald E Loth 46 F3
Garve Highld. 58 C3
Gatehouse of Fleet
 D & G. 41 G6
Gateshead Gatesd. 43 K5
Gaydon Warwks 22 E5
Gayton Norfk 24 E4
Gedney Drove End
 Lincs. 31 K6
Gedney Hill Lincs. 31 J8
Georgeham Devon. 4 D4
Gerrards Cross Bucks ... 15 G5
Gifford E Loth. 46 F3
Giggleswick N York 37 L6
Gillingham Dorset. 13 H8
Gillingham Medway. 10 F2
Gillingham Norfk. 25 L6
Gilling West N York. 38 B3
Gills Highld. 65 J1
Gilmerton P & K. 50 E4
Gilsland Nthumb. 42 E5
Gilwern Mons. 21 G8
Girton Cambs. 16 C2
Girvan S Ayrs 40 C3
Gisburn Lancs. 33 G2
Glamis Angus. 51 J3
Glanton Nthumb. 47 K7
Glapwell Derbys. 30 B3
Glasbury Powys 20 F6
Glasgow C Glas 45 J2
Glaston Rutlnd. 23 J1
Glastonbury Somset. 12 F7
Glemsford Suffk. 17 G3
Glenbarr Ag & B. 44 A4
Glenborrodale Highld. 52 D5
Glencaple D & G. 41 K5
Glencoe Highld. 53 H5
Glendaruel Ag & B. 49 H5
Glendevon P & K. 50 E6
Glenelg Highld. 57 H7
Glenfarg P & K. 51 G5
Glenfinnan Highld. 52 F3
Glenkindie Abers. 55 H3
Glenlivet Moray 59 K6
Glenluce D & G. 40 C6
Glen Maye IoM 36 b3
Glenridding Cumb. 37 G2
Glenrothes Fife 51 H6
Glentham Lincs. 35 G7
Glossop Derbys 33 J7
Gloucester Gloucs. 21 M7
Glyn Ceiriog Wrexhm 27 K6
Glyncorrwg Neath 19 L6
Glynde E Susx. 10 C7
Glynneath Neath. 19 L5
Glyntawe Powys. 20 C8
Gnosall Staffs 28 F7
Goathland N York. 39 H3
Goathurst Somset. 12 D7
Gobowen Shrops. 27 L6
Godalming Surrey 9 J2
Godmanchester
 Cambs. 23 M4
Godshill IoW 8 F7
Godstone Surrey 10 C3
Goginan Cerdgn 20 B3
Golborne Wigan 32 F6
Goldhanger Essex 17 G6
Golspie Highld. 64 E7
Gomshall Surrey 9 K2
Goole E R Yk. 34 E4
Goostrey Ches E 28 E3
Gordon Border. 47 G5
Gorebridge Mdloth 46 D4
Gorey Jersey 7 c1
Goring Oxon 14 D5
Gorran Haven Cnwll... 2 F6
Gorseinon Swans. 19 J6
Gosberton Lincs. 31 H6
Gosforth Cumb. 36 D3
Gosforth N u Ty 43 J5
Gosport Hants. 8 F5
Goudhurst Kent. 10 F4
Gourock Inver. 49 K5
Gowerton Swans. 19 J6
Goxhill N Linc. 35 H5

Grain Medway 11 G2
Grainthorpe Lincs. 35 K6
Grampound Cnwll 2 F6
Gramsdal W Isls 62 d9
Gramsdale W Isls 62 d9
Grandes Rocques
 Guern. 6 a1
Grange Cumb. 36 F2
Grangemouth Falk. 50 E8
Grange-over-Sands
 Cumb. 37 G5
Grantham Lincs. 30 F6
Grantown-on-Spey
 Highld. 59 J6
Grantshouse Border 47 H4
Grasmere Cumb. 37 G3
Grassington N York. 38 A6
Graveley Herts. 16 B4
Gravesend Kent. 10 E2
Grays Thurr. 10 E1
Great Ayton N York. 38 F3
Great Badminton
 S Glos 13 H3
Great Bardfield Essex. 16 E4
Great Barford Bed. 23 L5
Great Bircham Norfk. 24 E3
Great Blakenham
 Suffk. 17 J3
Great Casterton
 Rutlnd. 30 F8
Great Chesterford
 Essex. 16 D3
Great Dalby Leics 30 D7
Great Dunmow Essex... 16 E5
Great Durnford Wilts... 8 B3
Great Gidding Cambs ... 23 L3
Great Gransden
 Cambs. 16 B2
Greatham Hants 9 H3
Great Harwood
 Lancs. 33 G4
Great Haywood
 Staffs 29 G7
Great Hockham
 Norfk 25 G6
Great Kimble Bucks 14 F3
Great Langdale
 Cumb. 36 F3
Great Malvern Worcs. 21 L5
Great Massingham
 Norfk 24 E4
Great Missenden
 Bucks 14 F4
Great Notley Essex. 16 E5
Great Ponton Lincs. 30 F6
Great Sampford
 Essex. 16 E4
Great Saughall
 Ches W. 28 B3
Great Shefford
 W Berk 14 B6
Great Shelford
 Cambs. 16 C3
Great Smeaton
 N York 38 D3
Great Tew Oxon. 22 E7
Great Torrington
 Devon 4 E5
Great Wakering
 Essex. 17 G8
Great Waltham
 Essex. 16 E6
Great Witley Worcs. 21 L4
Great Yarmouth
 Norfk 25 L5
Great Yeldham Essex. 16 F4
Greenfield Flints. 27 K3
Green Hammerton
 N York 38 E7
Greenhead Nthumb. 42 E5
Greenhow Hill N York ... 38 B6
Greenlaw Border 47 G5
Greenloaning P & K 50 D6
Greenock Inver. 49 L5
Greenodd Cumb. 36 F5
Greetham Rutlnd. 30 F7
Gresford Wrexhm 27 L4
Greta Bridge Dur. 38 B3
Gretna D & G 42 B5
Gretna Green D & G 42 B5
Greystoke Cumb. 42 C8
Grimsby NE Lin 35 J5
Grimsthorpe Lincs. 31 G7
Grindleford Derbys 29 J3
Gringley on the Hill
 Notts. 34 E7
Groby Leics 30 B8
Grosmont Mons. 21 H7
Grouville Jersey 7 c2
Grove Oxon 14 B5
Guardbridge Fife 51 J5

Guestling Green
E Susx 11 G6
Guildford Surrey 9 K2
Guisborough R & Cl ..38 F2
Guiseley Leeds 33 K3
Guist Norfk 25 G4
Gullane E Loth 46 E2
Gunness N Linc 34 K3
Gunnislake Cnwll 3 K4
Gunthorpe Notts 30 D5
Gurnard IoW 8 E6
Gussage All Saints
Dorset 8 A5
Gutcher Shet 61 d2
Guyhirn Cambs 24 B5
Gweek Cnwll 2 D7
Gwernymynydd
Flints 27 K4
Gwithian Cnwll 2 C6
Gwyddelwern
Denbgs 27 J5

H

Hackland Ork 65 b3
Hackness N York 39 J4
Hackney Gt Lon 15 K5
Haddenham Bucks 14 E3
Haddenham Cambs 24 C7
Haddington E Loth 46 F3
Haddiscoe Norfk 25 L6
Hadleigh Suffk 17 H3
Hadlow Kent 10 E4
Hagworthingham
Lincs 31 J3
Hailsham E Susx 10 E7
Halberton Devon 5 J4
Hales Norfk 25 K6
Halesowen Dudley 22 A3
Halesworth Suffk 25 K7
Halifax Calder 33 K4
Halkirk Highld 65 G2
Halstead Essex 16 F4
Halstead Kent 10 D3
Haltwhistle Nthumb ..42 E5
Halwell Devon 6 B6
Halwill Junction
Devon 4 D7
Hambledon Hants 9 G4
Hamble-le-Rice
Hants 8 E5
Hambleton Lancs 32 D3
Hamilton S Lans 45 K3
Hammersmith Gt Lon ..15 J6
Hampstead Norreys
W Berk 14 C6
Hampsthwaite
N York 38 C7
Hamstead Marshall
W Berk 14 B7
Hamstreet Kent 11 H5
Handcross W Susx 10 B5
Handley Ches W 28 C4
Hanley C Stke 28 F5
Happisburgh Norfk 25 K3
Harbertonford
Devon 6 B6
Hardwicke Gloucs 13 H1
Hare Street Herts 16 C4
Harewood Leeds 33 L3
Harewood End
Herefs 21 J7
Harlech Gwynd 26 E6
Harleston Norfk 25 J7
Harlosh Highld 56 C5
Harlow Essex 16 C6
Harlyn Cnwll 2 E4
Haroldswick Shet 61 d1
Harpenden Herts 15 H3
Harrogate N York 33 L2
Harrold Bed 23 K5
Harrow Gt Lon 15 H5
Harston Cambs 16 C3
Hartburn Nthumb 43 H3
Hartest Suffk 17 G3
Hartfield E Susx 10 D5
Hartington Derbys 29 H4
Hartland Devon 4 C5
Hartlepool Hartpl 43 M8
Hartley Wintney
Hants 14 E7
Hartpury Gloucs 21 L7
Harvington Worcs 22 B5
Harwich Essex 17 K4
Haseley Warwks 22 D4
Haslemere Surrey 9 J3
Hastings E Susx 10 F7
Hatch Beauchamp
Somset 12 D8

Hatfield Donc 34 D5
Hatfield Herts 15 J3
Hatfield Broad Oak
Essex 16 D5
Hatfield Heath Essex .16 D5
Hatfield Peverel
Essex 16 F6
Hatherleigh Devon 4 E6
Hathern Leics 30 B7
Hathersage Derbys ...29 J2
Hatton Abers 61 H5
Havant Hants 9 G5
Havenstreet IoW 8 F6
Haverfordwest
Pembks 18 C5
Haverhill Suffk 16 E3
Hawarden Flints 27 L3
Hawes N York 37 L4
Hawick Border 46 F7
Hawkedon Suffk 16 F3
Hawkhurst Kent 10 F5
Hawkinge Kent 11 K4
Hawkshead Cumb 37 G4
Hawnby N York 38 E4
Haworth C Brad 33 J3
Haxby C York 38 F7
Haxey N Linc 34 E6
Haydon Bridge
Nthumb 42 F5
Hayle Cnwll 2 C6
Hay-on-Wye Powys 21 G6
Haywards Heath
W Susx 10 B6
Hazel Grove Stockp ..28 F2
Heacham Norfk 24 D3
Headcorn Kent 11 G4
Heanor Derbys 29 L5
Heath Derbys 29 L3
Heathfield E Susx 10 E6
Heath Hayes &
Wimblebury
Staffs 29 G8
Heckington Lincs 31 G5
Hedge End Hants 8 E4
Hednesford Staffs ...29 G8
Hedon E R Yk 35 H4
Helensburgh Ag & B ..49 L5
Hellifield N York 37 L7
Helmingham Suffk 17 K2
Helmsdale Highld 65 G6
Helmsley N York 38 E5
Helpringham Lincs 31 G5
Helsby Ches W 28 C3
Helston Cnwll 2 C7
Hemel Hempstead
Herts 15 H3
Hempnall Norfk 25 J6
Hemsby Norfk 25 L4
Hemsworth Wakefd 34 B5
Hemyock Devon 5 K6
Hendy Carmth 19 J6
Henfield W Susx 9 L4
Henham Essex 16 D4
Henley-in-Arden
Warwks 22 C4
Henley-on-Thames
Oxon 14 E5
Henllan Denbgs 27 J3
Henlow C Beds 23 L6
Henstead Suffk 25 L7
Henstridge Somset 7 K1
Hereford Herefs 21 J6
Hermitage W Berk 14 C6
Herne Bay Kent 11 J2
Hersden Kent 11 K3
Herstmonceux
E Susx 10 E6
Hertford Herts 15 K3
Hessle E R Yk 35 G4
Heswall Wirral 27 L2
Hethersett Norfk 25 H5
Heversham Cumb 37 H5
Hexham Nthumb 43 G5
Hexworthy Devon 3 M4
Heybrook Bay Devon ...3 K6
Heysham Lancs 37 G7
Heytesbury Wilts 13 J6
Hibaldstow N Linc 35 G6
Hickstead W Susx 10 B6
Higham Ferrers
Nhants 23 K4
Highampton Devon 4 E6
High Bentham N York ..37 K6
Highbridge Somset 12 D6
Highclere Hants 14 B7
High Ercall Wrekin ...28 D7
Higher Town IoS 2 b1
High Halden Kent 11 G5
High Hesket Cumb 42 C7
Highley Shrops 21 L3
High Roding Essex 16 E5

Highworth Swindn ...13 M3
High Wycombe
Bucks 14 F4
Hildenborough Kent ..10 D4
Hill Brow Hants 9 H3
Hill of Fearn Highld .59 G2
Hillswick Shet 61 b3
Hilmarton Wilts 13 K4
Hilton Derbys 29 J6
Hinckley Leics 22 E2
Hinderwell N York 39 G2
Hindhead Surrey 9 J3
Hindon Wilts 13 J7
Hingham Norfk 25 G5
Hipswell N York 38 B4
Hirwaun Rhondd 12 A2
Histon Cambs 16 C2
Hitcham Suffk 17 H3
Hitchin Herts 23 M7
Hockley Essex 17 G7
Hockliffe C Beds 23 K7
Hoddesdon Herts 15 K3
Hodnet Shrops 28 D6
Hogsthorpe Lincs 31 L3
Holbeach Lincs 31 J7
Holbeton Devon 3 L5
Holbrook Suffk 17 J4
Holbury Hants 8 E5
Holkham Norfk 24 E2
Hollingbourne Kent ..11 G3
Holmbury St Mary
Surrey 9 L2
Holmes Chapel
Ches E 28 E3
Holme upon
Spalding Moor
E R Yk 34 E3
Holmfirth Kirk 33 K6
Holmrook Cumb 36 D4
Holne Devon 6 A5
Holsworthy Devon 4 C6
Holt Norfk 25 H3
Holt Wilts 13 J5
Holt Wrexhm 28 B4
Holt Heath Worcs 21 M6
Holton le Clay Lincs .35 J6
Holyhead IoA 26 B2
Holy Island Nthumb ..47 L5
Holytown N Lans 45 L2
Holywell Dorset 7 J2
Holywell Flints 27 K3
Homersfield Suffk 25 J7
Honingham Norfk 25 H5
Honington Suffk 24 F7
Honiton Devon 6 E4
Hook Hants 14 E7
Hoo St Werburgh
Medway 10 F2
Hope Derbys 29 J2
Hope Devon 6 A7
Hope Flints 27 L4
Hope Bowdler
Shrops 21 J2
Hopeman Moray 59 K3
Hope under
Dinmore Herefs 21 J5
Hopton on Sea
Norfk 25 M5
Horam E Susx 10 D6
Horley Surrey 10 B4
Hornby Lancs 37 J6
Horncastle Lincs 31 H3
Horndean Hants 9 G4
Horns Cross Devon 4 D5
Hornsea E R Yk 35 H3
Horrabridge Devon 3 L4
Horsey Norfk 25 L4
Horsham W Susx 9 L3
Horsley Nthumb 43 H5
Horton Dorset 8 B5
Horton Somset 6 F1
Horton-cum-Studley
Oxon 14 D3
Horton in
Ribblesdale
N York 37 L6
Horwich Bolton 32 F5
Hoton Leics 30 C7
Houghton-le-Spring
Sundld 43 K6
Houghton on the
Hill Leics 23 G1
Hounslow Gt Lon 15 H6
Houton Ork 65 b4
Hove Br & H 10 B7
Hovingham N York 38 F5
Howden E R Yk 34 F4
Hoxne Suffk 25 J7
Hoylake Wirral 32 B7
Hoyland Nether
Barns 34 B6

Hucknall Notts 30 B5
Huddersfield Kirk ...33 K5
Hugh Town IoS 2 a2
Hull, Kingston upon
C Kuh 35 G4
Humberston NE Lin ...35 J6
Humbie E Loth 46 E4
Humby Border 47 G5
Hungerford W Berk ...14 B6
Hunmanby N York 39 K5
Hunstanton Norfk 24 D2
Huntingdon Cambs 23 M3
Huntley Gloucs 21 L7
Huntly Abers 60 C5
Hursley Hants 8 E4
Hurstbourne Priors
Hants 8 E2
Hurstbourne Tarrant
Hants 14 B7
Hurst Green E Susx ..10 F5
Hurst Green Lancs ...32 F3
Hurstpierpoint
W Susx 10 B6
Hurworth-on-Tees
Darltn 38 C3
Husbands Bosworth
Leics 23 G2
Husborne Crawley
C Beds 23 K6
Huttoft Lincs 31 L3
Hutton-le-Hole
N York 39 G4
Hyde Tamesd 33 H7
Hynish Ag & B 48 b3
Hythe Hants 8 E5
Hythe Kent 11 J5

I

Ibstock Leics 29 K8
Ideford Devon 6 C4
Ilchester Somset 12 F8
Ilfracombe Devon 4 E3
Ilkeston Derbys 29 L5
Ilkley C Brad 33 K3
Ilminster Somset 7 G1
Immingham NE Lin 35 H5
Immingham Dock
NE Lin 35 H5
Inchnadamph
Highld 63 H5
Ingatestone Essex ...16 E7
Ingham Lincs 30 F2
Ingleton N York 37 K6
Ingoldmells Lincs 31 L3
Inkberrow Worcs 22 B5
Innellan Ag & B 49 K6
Innerleithen Border ..46 D6
Insch Abers 60 D6
Instow Devon 4 D4
Inveralligin Abers ...61 G3
Inveran Highld 64 C7
Inveraray Ag & B 49 J3
Inverasdale Highld ...57 H2
Inverbervie Abers ...55 L6
Invergarry Highld 53 K2
Invergordon Highld ...58 F3
Invergowrie P & K 51 H4
Inverinate Highld 57 J6
Inverkeilor Angus ...51 L2
Inverkeithing Fife ..46 B2
Inverkeithny Abers ..60 D5
Inverkip Inver 49 K6
Invermoriston
Highld 58 D7
Inverness Highld 58 F5
Inverurie Abers 55 L3
Ipplepen Devon 6 B5
Ipstones Staffs 29 G5
Ipswich Suffk 17 J3
Irchester Nhants 23 J4
Ireby Cumb 42 A7
Ironbridge Wrekin ...21 K1
Irthlingborough
Nhants 23 K3
Irvine N Ayrs 45 G4
Isle of Whithorn
D & G 40 F7
Isleornsay Highld 57 G7
Islington Gt Lon 15 K5
Itchen Abbas Hants ...8 F3
Iver Bucks 15 G5
Ivinghoe Bucks 15 G3
Ivybridge Devon 3 M5
Iwade Kent 11 G2
Iwerne Minster
Dorset 7 L1
Ixworth Suffk 25 G8

J

Jarrow S Tyne 43 K5
Jedburgh Border 47 G7
Jerbourg Guern 6 b2
Jevington E Susx 10 D7
John o' Groats Highld .. 65 J1
Johnshaven Abers 55 L7
Johnston Pembks 18 C5
Johnstone Rens 49 M6
Jurby IoM 36 c1

K

Kames Ag & B 49 H6
Keelby Lincs 35 H5
Kegworth Leics 30 B6
Keighley C Brad 33 J3
Keiss Highld 65 J2
Keith Moray 60 D4
Keld N York 37 L3
Kelham Notts 30 D4
Kelso Border 47 G6
Kelvedon Essex 17 G5
Kemble Gloucs 13 K2
Kemnay Abers 55 K3
Kempston Bed 23 K5
Kendal Cumb 37 H4
Kenilworth Warwks 22 D3
Kenmore P & K 50 D3
Kennacraig Ag & B 49 G6
Kennford Devon 6 C3
Kenninghall Norfk 25 G7
Kentallen Highld 53 G5
Kentford Suffk 16 F2
Kenton Devon 6 C4
Kerry Powys 20 F2
Kessingland Suffk 25 L6
Keswick Cumb 36 F2
Kettering Nhants 23 J3
Kettlewell N York 37 M6
Ketton Rutlnd 23 K1
Keymer W Susx 10 B6
Keynsham BaNES 13 G4
Keyston Cambs 23 K3
Keyworth Notts 30 C6
Kibworth Harcourt
Leics 23 G2
Kidderminster
Worcs 21 M3
Kidlington Oxon 14 C3
Kidsgrove Staffs 28 F4
Kidwelly Carmth 19 G5
Kielder Nthumb 42 D3
Kilberry Ag & B 48 F6
Kilbirnie N Ayrs 45 G3
Kilburn Derbys 29 K5
Kilburn N York 38 E5
Kilchattan Ag & B 44 E3
Kilchoan Highld 52 C4
Kilchrenan Ag & B 49 J2
Kilcreggan Ag & B 49 K5
Kildale N York 38 F3
Kildrummy Abers 55 H3
Kildwick N York 33 J3
Kilfinan Ag & B 49 H5
Kilgetty Pembks 18 E5
Kilham E R Yk 39 K6
Kilkenzie Ag & B 44 B5
Kilkhampton Cnwll 4 C6
Killearn Stirlg 50 B7
Killiecrankie P & K 54 D7
Killin Stirlg 50 B4
Kilmacolm Inver 49 L6
Kilmany Fife 51 J5
Kilmarnock E Ayrs 45 H4
Kilmartin Ag & B 49 G4
Kilmaurs E Ayrs 45 H4
Kilmelford Ag & B 49 G3
Kilmorack Highld 58 D5
Kilninver Ag & B 49 G2
Kilsyth N Lans 50 C8
Kilve Somset 5 K3
Kilwinning N Ayrs 45 G4
Kimberley Norfk 25 H5
Kimbolton Cambs 23 L4
Kinbrace Highld 64 E5
Kincardine Fife 50 E7
Kincardine O'Neil
Abers 55 J4
Kincraig Highld 54 C4
Kineton Warwks 22 E5
Kingsbarns Fife 51 K5
Kingsbridge Devon 6 B7
Kingsbury Warwks 22 D2
Kingsclere Hants 14 C7
King's Cliffe Nhants 23 K1
Kingsdown Kent 11 L4

Kingsfold W Susx 9 L3
Kingskerswell Devon 6 C5
Kingsland Herefs 21 H4
Kings Langley
Herts 15 H4
Kingsley Staffs 29 G5
King's Lynn Norfk 24 D4
King's Mills Guern 6 a2
Kingsnorth Kent 11 H4
King's Somborne
Hants 8 D3
King's Stag Dorset 7 K2
King's Stanley
Gloucs 13 H2
Kingsteignton
Devon 6 C4
Kingstone Herefs 21 H6
Kingston on Spey
Moray 59 L3
Kingston upon Hull
C KuH 35 G4
Kingston upon
Thames Gt Lon 15 J6
Kingswear Devon 6 C6
Kings Worthy Hants 8 E3
Kington Herefs 21 G5
Kingussie Highld 54 B4
Kinlochbervie
Highld 63 H3
Kinlocheil Highld 53 G3
Kinlochewe Highld 57 J3
Kinlochleven Highld 53 J5
Kinloch Rannoch
P & K 50 C2
Kinloss Moray 59 J3
Kinneff Abers 55 L6
Kinross P & K 50 F6
Kintbury W Berk 14 B6
Kintore Abers 55 L3
Kippen Stirlg 50 C7
Kirby Misperton
N York 39 G5
Kirby Muxloe Leics 22 F1
Kirkabister Shet 61 c6
Kirkbean D & G 41 K6
Kirkbride Cumb 42 A6
Kirkburton Kirk 33 K5
Kirkby Knows 32 D6
Kirkby in Ashfield
Notts 30 B4
Kirkby Lonsdale
Cumb 37 J5
Kirkby Malzeard
N York 38 C5
Kirkbymoorside
N York 39 G5
Kirkby Stephen
Cumb 37 K3
Kirkcaldy Fife 51 H7
Kirkcolm D & G 40 B5
Kirkconnel D & G 45 K6
Kirkcowan D & G 40 D5
Kirkcudbright D & G 41 G6
Kirkham Lancs 32 D4
Kirkhill Highld 58 E5
Kirkinner D & G 40 E6
Kirkintilloch E Duns 45 K1
Kirk Langley Derbys 29 K6
Kirk Michael IoM 36 b2
Kirkmichael P & K 50 F2
Kirkmichael S Ayrs 45 G6
Kirknewton Nthumb 47 J6
Kirkoswald Cumb 42 D7
Kirkoswald S Ayrs 44 F6
Kirkpatrick-Fleming
D & G 42 B5
Kirkton of Skene
Abers 55 L4
Kirkwall IoA 65 c4
Kirkwhelpington
Nthumb 43 H4
Kirriemuir Angus 51 J2
Kirton Lincs 31 J6
Kirton in Lindsey
N Linc 34 F6
Kislingbury Nhants 23 H4
Knaresborough
N York 38 D7
Knarsdale Nthumb 42 E6
Knebworth Herts 15 J2
Knighton Powys 21 G3
Knightwick Worcs 21 L5
Knockan Highld 63 H6
Knockin Shrops 27 L7
Knottingley Wakefd 34 C4
Knowl Hill W & M 14 F5
Knutsford Ches E 28 E3
Kyleakin Highld 57 G6
Kyle of Lochalsh
Highld 57 G6
Kylerhea Highld 57 G7

L

Laceby NE Lin 35 H6
Ladock Cnwll 2 E5
Ladybank Fife 51 H5
Laggan Highld 54 A5
La Greve de Lecq
Jersey 7 a1
Laide Highld 62 E8
Lairg Highld 64 C6
Lakenheath Suffk 24 E7
Lamberhurst Kent 10 E5
Lambourn W Berk 14 B6
Lamerton Devon 3 K3
Lamington S Lans 46 A6
Lamlash N Ayrs 44 D5
Lampeter Cerdgn 19 J2
Lamport Nhants 23 H3
Lanark S Lans 45 M4
Lancaster Lancs 37 H6
Lanchester Dur 43 J6
Lancing W Susx 9 L5
L'Ancresse Guern 6 b1
Landrake Cnwll 3 J5
Langham Rutlnd 30 F8
Langholm D & G 42 B4
Langport Somset 12 E8
Langthwaite N York 38 A3
Langtoft E R Yk 39 J6
Langton Matravers
Dorset 8 A7
Langwathby Cumb 42 D7
Langworth Lincs 31 G3
Lanivet Cnwll 3 G4
Lapford Devon 5 G6
Largoward Fife 51 J6
Largs N Ayrs 44 F2
Larkhall S Lans 45 L3
Larkhill Wilts 8 B2
Lastingham N York 39 G4
Latchingdon Essex 17 G7
Latheron Highld 65 H4
Lauder Border 46 F5
Laugharne Carmth 18 F5
Launceston Cnwll 3 J3
Laurencekirk Abers 55 K6
Laurieston D & G 41 G5
Lavenham Suffk 17 G3
Lawers P & K 50 C3
Laxey IoM 36 c3
Laxfield Suffk 25 K8
Lazonby Cumb 42 D7
Leadenham Lincs 30 F5
Leaden Roding Essex .. 16 E6
Leadgate Dur 43 J6
Leadhills S Lans 45 M6
Leamington Spa
Warwks 22 D4
Leatherhead Surrey 15 J7
Lechlade on Thames
Gloucs 13 M2
Ledbury Herefs 21 L6
Lee Devon 4 E3
Leebotwood Shrops 21 J1
Leeds Leeds 33 L4
Leek Staffs 29 G4
Leeming Bar N York 38 C4
Lee-on-the-Solent
Hants 8 F5
Legbourne Lincs 31 J2
Leicester C Leic 23 G1
Leigh Kent 10 D4
Leigh Wigan 32 F6
Leigh Sinton Worcs 21 L5
Leighton Buzzard
C Beds 23 J7
Leintwardine Herefs ... 21 H3
Leiston Suffk 17 M2
Lelant Cnwll 2 C6
Lendalfoot S Ayrs 40 C3
Lenham Kent 11 G3
Lennoxtown E Duns 50 B8
Leominster Herefs 21 J4
L'Eree Guern 6 a2
Lerwick Shet 61 c6
Leslie Abers 60 D6
Leslie Fife 51 H6
Lesmahagow S Lans .. 45 L4
Leswalt D & G 40 B5
L'Etacq Jersey 7 a1
Letchworth Garden
City Herts 16 B4
Letham Angus 51 K3
Letterston Pembks 18 C4
Leuchars Fife 51 J5
Leven E R Yk 35 H3
Leven Fife 51 J6
Levens Cumb 37 H5
Leverburgh W Isls 62 e7
Lewes E Susx 10 C7

Leyburn N York 38 B4
Leyland Lancs 32 E5
Leysdown-on-Sea
Kent 11 H2
Lhanbryde Moray 59 L3
Libberton S Lans 46 A5
Lichfield Staffs 29 H8
Lidgate Suffk 16 F2
Lifton Devon 3 J3
Lightwater Surrey 15 G7
Lilliesleaf Border 46 F7
Limpley Stoke Wilts 13 H5
Lincoln Lincs 30 F3
Lindale Cumb 37 G5
Lingfield Surrey 10 C4
Linlithgow W Loth 46 A3
Linton Cambs 16 D3
Linton Kent 10 F4
Liphook Hants 9 H3
Liskeard Cnwll 3 H4
Liss Hants 9 H3
Lissington Lincs 31 G2
Litcham Norfk 24 F4
Litchfield Hants 14 C7
Little Abington
Cambs 16 D3
Little Berkhamsted
Herts 15 K3
Littleborough Rochdl .. 33 H5
Little Brickhill M Keyn .. 23 J6
Little Bytham Lincs 30 F7
Little Clacton Essex 17 J5
Little Gaddesden
Herts 15 G3
Littlehampton
W Susx 9 K5
Littleport Cambs 24 D6
Little Stretton Shrops .. 21 H2
Little Torrington
Devon 4 E5
Little Walsingham
Norfk 25 G3
Liverpool Lpool 32 C7
Livingston W Loth 46 B3
Lizard Cnwll 2 D8
Llanaelhaearn
Gwynd 26 C5
Llanarmon Dyffryn
Ceiriog Wrexhm 27 K6
Llanarthne Carmth 19 H4
Llanbedr Gwynd 26 E6
Llanbedr-Dyffryn-
Clwyd Denbgs 27 K4
Llanbedrog Gwynd 26 C6
Llanberis Gwynd 26 E4
Llanbister Powys 20 F3
Llanbrynmair Powys ... 20 D1
Llanddarog Carmth 19 H5
Llandderfel Gwynd 27 H6
Llanddulas Conwy 27 H3
Llandeilo Carmth 19 J4
Llandinam Powys 20 E2
Llandissilio Pembks 18 E4
Llandovery Carmth 19 K3
Llandre Cerdgn 20 B2
Llandrillo Denbgs 27 J6
Llandrindod Wells
Powys 20 E4
Llandrinio Powys 27 L7
Llandudno Conwy 27 G2
Llandwrog Gwynd 26 D4
Llandybie Carmth 19 J5
Llandysul Cerdgn 19 G3
Llanelli Carmth 19 H6
Llanerchymedd IoA 26 D2
Llanerfyl Powys 27 J8
Llanfachraeth IoA 26 C2
Llanfair Caereinion
Powys 27 J8
Llanfair Dyffryn
Clwyd Denbgs 27 J4
Llanfairfechan
Conwy 26 F2
Llanfair P G IoA 26 D3
Llanfair Talhaiarn
Conwy 27 H3
Llanfair Waterdine
Shrops 21 G3
Llanfarian Cerdgn 20 A3
Llanfyllin Powys 27 K7
Llangadfan Powys 27 H8
Llangadog Carmth 19 K4
Llangammarch Wells
Powys 20 D5
Llangedwyn Powys 27 K7
Llangefni IoA 26 D3
Llangeinor Brdgnd 19 L7
Llangeler Carmth 19 G3
Llangennith Swans 19 G6
Llangernyw Conwy 27 G3
Llangoed IoA 26 E2

Place	County	Page	Grid
Llangollen	Denbgs	27	K5
Llangors	Powys	20	F7
Llangrannog	Cerdgn	18	F2
Llangurig	Powys	20	D3
Llangynidr	Powys	20	F7
Llangynog	Powys	27	J7
Llanhamlach	Powys	20	E7
Llanharan	Rhondd	12	B3
Llanidloes	Powys	20	D2
Llanilar	Cerdgn	20	B3
Llanllechid	Gwynd	26	E3
Llannefydd	Conwy	27	H3
Llanrhaeadr-ym-Mochnant	Powys	27	J7
Llanrhidian	Swans	19	H6
Llanrhystud	Cerdgn	20	A4
Llanrug	Gwynd	26	E4
Llanrwst	Conwy	27	G4
Llansanffraid Glan Conwy	Conwy	27	G3
Llansannan	Conwy	27	H3
Llansantffraid	Cerdgn	19	H1
Llansantffraid-ym-Mechain	Powys	27	K7
Llansawel	Carmth	19	J3
Llansteffan	Carmth	19	G5
Llanthony	Mons	21	G7
Llantrisant	Rhondd	12	B3
Llantwit Major	V Glam	5	J1
Llanuwchllyn	Gwynd	27	G6
Llanvetherine	Mons	21	H8
Llanvihangel Crucorney	Mons	21	G7
Llanwddyn	Powys	27	J7
Llanwnda	Gwynd	26	D4
Llanwrda	Carmth	19	K3
Llanwrtyd Wells	Powys	20	D5
Llanybydder	Carmth	19	H2
Llanymynech	Powys	27	L7
Llanystumdwy	Gwynd	26	D6
Llay	Wrexhm	27	L4
Llechryd	Cerdgn	18	F3
Llwyngwril	Gwynd	26	E8
Llwynmawr	Wrexhm	27	K6
Llynclys	Shrops	27	L7
Llyswen	Powys	20	F6
Lochailort	Highld	52	E3
Lochaline	Highld	52	D6
Locharbriggs	D & G	41	K4
Lochawe	Ag & B	53	H7
Loch Baghasdail	W Isls	62	C12
Lochboisdale	W Isls	62	c12
Lochbuie	Ag & B	52	D7
Lochcarron	Highld	57	H5
Lochdonhead	Ag & B	52	E7
Lochearnhead	Stirlg	50	B4
Lochgair	Ag & B	49	H4
Lochgilphead	Ag & B	49	G4
Lochgoilhead	Ag & B	49	K3
Lochinver	Highld	63	G5
Lochmaben	D & G	41	L4
Lochmaddy	W Isls	62	d8
Loch nam Madadh	W Isls	62	d8
Lochranza	N Ayrs	44	D3
Lochwinnoch	Rens	45	G2
Lockerbie	D & G	41	L4
Lockton	N York	39	H4
Loddon	Norfk	25	K6
Lofthouse	N York	38	B6
Loftus	R & Cl	39	G2
London	Gt Lon	15	J5
London Colney	Herts	15	J4
Long Ashton	N Som	12	F4
Long Bennington	Lincs	30	E5
Long Buckby	Nhants	23	G4
Longburton	Dorset	7	J1
Long Compton	Warwks	22	D6
Long Crendon	Bucks	14	E3
Long Eaton	Derbys	30	B6
Longford	Gloucs	21	M7
Longformacus	Border	47	G4
Long Framlington	Nthumb	43	J2
Longham	Dorset	8	B6
Longhorsley	Nthumb	43	J3
Longhoughton	Nthumb	47	M7
Long Itchington	Warwks	22	E4
Long Lawford	Warwks	22	F3
Long Marston	N York	34	C2
Long Melford	Suffk	17	G3
Longniddry	E Loth	46	E3
Longnor	Shrops	21	J1
Longnor	Staffs	29	H4
Long Preston	N York	37	L2
Longridge	Lancs	32	F3
Longridge	W Loth	45	M2
Longside	Abers	61	G5
Long Stratton	Norfk	25	J6
Long Sutton	Lincs	31	K7
Long Sutton	Somset	12	F8
Longton	Lancs	32	D4
Longtown	Cumb	42	B5
Longville in the Dale	Shrops	21	J2
Looe	Cnwll	3	H5
Lossiemouth	Moray	59	K3
Lostwithiel	Cnwll	3	G5
Loughborough	Leics	30	B7
Louth	Lincs	31	J2
Lowdham	Notts	30	C3
Lower Diabaig	Highld	57	H4
Lower Dicker	E Susx	10	D6
Lower Peover	Ches E	28	E3
Lower Swell	Gloucs	22	C7
Lowestoft	Suffk	25	M6
Loweswater	Cumb	36	E2
Lowick	Nhants	23	K3
Lowick	Nthumb	47	K5
Low Row	N York	37	M4
Lubenham	Leics	23	H2
Ludborough	Lincs	35	J7
Ludgershall	Wilts	8	D2
Ludham	Norfk	25	K4
Ludlow	Shrops	21	J3
Lugton	E Ayrs	45	H3
Lugwardine	Herefs	21	J6
Lumphanan	Abers	55	J4
Lumsden	Abers	55	H3
Lunan	Angus	51	L2
Lupton	Cumb	37	H5
Luss	Ag & B	49	L4
Lusta	Highld	56	C4
Luton	Luton	15	H2
Lutterworth	Leics	22	F2
Lybster	Highld	65	H4
Lydbury North	Shrops	21	H2
Lydd	Kent	11	H6
Lydford	Devon	3	L3
Lydford on Fosse	Somset	12	F7
Lydham	Shrops	21	G2
Lydney	Gloucs	13	G2
Lyme Regis	Dorset	7	G3
Lyminge	Kent	11	J4
Lymington	Hants	8	D6
Lymm	Warrtn	28	E2
Lympne	Kent	11	J5
Lyndhurst	Hants	8	D5
Lyneham	Wilts	13	K4
Lyness	Ork	65	b5
Lyng	Somset	12	E8
Lynmouth	Devon	5	G3
Lynton	Devon	4	F3
Lyonshall	Herefs	21	G5
Lytham St Anne's	Lancs	32	C4
Lythe	N York	39	H3

M

Place	County	Page	Grid
Mablethorpe	Lincs	31	K2
Macclesfield	Ches E	28	F3
Macduff	Abers	60	E3
Machrihanish	Ag & B	44	A5
Machynlleth	Powys	20	C1
Macmerry	E Loth	46	E3
Maentwrog	Gwynd	26	F5
Maerdy	Rhondd	12	B3
Maesteg	Brdgnd	19	L7
Maghull	Sefton	32	D6
Maiden Bradley	Wilts	13	H7
Maidencombe	Torbay	6	C5
Maidenhead	W & M	14	F5
Maiden Newton	Dorset	7	J3
Maidstone	Kent	10	F3
Mainsriddle	D & G	41	K6
Malborough	Devon	6	A7
Maldon	Essex	17	G6
Malham	N York	37	L6
Mallaig	Highld	52	D2
Mallwyd	Gwynd	27	G8
Malmesbury	Wilts	13	J3
Malpas	Ches W	28	C5
Maltby	Rothm	34	C7
Malton	N York	39	G6
Malvern Wells	Worcs	21	L6
Manaccan	Cnwll	2	D7
Manchester	Manch	33	G6
Manea	Cambs	24	C6
Manningtree	Essex	17	J4
Manorbier	Pembks	18	D6
Mansfield	Notts	30	B4
Marazanvose	Cnwll	2	E5
Marazion	Cnwll	2	B7
March	Cambs	24	B6
Marchwiel	Wrexhm	28	B5
Marden	Kent	10	F4
Mareham le Fen	Lincs	31	J4
Margaretting	Essex	16	E6
Margate	Kent	11	L2
Mark	Somset	12	E6
Mark Cross	E Susx	10	E5
Market Bosworth	Leics	22	E1
Market Deeping	Lincs	31	G8
Market Drayton	Shrops	28	D6
Market Harborough	Leics	23	H2
Market Lavington	Wilts	13	K6
Market Rasen	Lincs	35	H7
Market Warsop	Notts	30	C3
Market Weighton	E R Yk	34	F3
Markfield	Leics	30	B8
Markham Moor	Notts	30	D3
Marksbury	BaNES	13	G5
Marks Tey	Essex	17	G5
Marlborough	Wilts	13	M4
Marloes	Pembks	18	B5
Marlow	Bucks	14	F5
Marnhull	Dorset	7	K1
Marshfield	S Glos	13	H4
Marsh Gibbon	Bucks	14	D2
Marske-by-the-Sea	R & Cl	38	F2
Martin	Lincs	31	G4
Martinstown	Dorset	7	J3
Martlesham Heath	Suffk	17	K3
Martock	Somset	7	H1
Marton	Warwks	22	E4
Marykirk	Abers	51	K7
Maryport	Cumb	41	K7
Mary Tavy	Devon	3	L3
Marywell	Abers	55	J5
Masham	N York	38	C5
Matfield	Kent	10	E4
Matlock	Derbys	29	K4
Mattingley	Hants	14	E7
Maud	Abers	60	F4
Maughold	IoM	36	d2
Maulden	C Beds	23	K6
Mawgan Porth	Cnwll	2	E4
Mawnan Smith	Cnwll	2	D7
Maybole	S Ayrs	45	G6
Mayfield	E Susx	10	E5
Mayfield	Staffs	29	H5
Meare	Somset	12	F6
Measham	Leics	29	K8
Medstead	Hants	9	G3
Meeth	Devon	4	E6
Meifod	Powys	27	K8
Meigle	P & K	51	H3
Melbourn	Cambs	16	C3
Melbourne	Derbys	29	K7
Meliden	Denbgs	27	J2
Melksham	Wilts	13	J5
Melling	Lancs	37	J6
Melmerby	Cumb	42	D7
Melrose	Border	46	F6
Meltham	Kirk	33	K5
Melton	E R Yk	34	F4
Melton Constable	Norfk	25	H3
Melton Mowbray	Leics	30	D7
Melvaig	Highld	57	G2
Melvich	Highld	64	G2
Memsie	Abers	61	G3
Memus	Angus	51	J2
Menai Bridge	IoA	26	E3
Mentmore	Bucks	14	F2
Meopham	Kent	10	E2
Mere	Wilts	13	H7
Meriden	Solhll	22	D3
Merthyr Tydfil	Myr Td	12	B3
Merton	Devon	4	E6
Messingham	N Linc	34	F6
Metfield	Suffk	25	K7
Methil	Fife	51	J6
Methlick	Abers	60	F5
Methven	P & K	50	F4
Methwold	Norfk	24	E6
Mevagissey	Cnwll	2	F6
Mexborough	Donc	34	B6
Miabhig	W Isls	62	f3
Miavaig	W Isls	62	f3
Micheldever	Hants	8	F2
Mickleton	Dur	37	M2
Mickleton	Gloucs	22	C6
Midbea	Ork	65	C2
Middleham	N York	38	B4
Middle Rasen	Lincs	35	G7
Middlesbrough	Middsb	38	E2
Middleton Cheney	Nhants	22	F6
Middleton-in-Teesdale	Dur	37	M2
Middleton-on-Sea	W Susx	9	J5
Middleton on the Wolds	E R Yk	34	F2
Middleton Stoney	Oxon	14	C2
Middle Town	IoS	2	a2
Middle Wallop	Hants	8	D3
Middlewich	Ches E	28	E3
Middlezoy	Somset	12	E7
Midhurst	W Susx	9	J4
Midsomer Norton	BaNES	13	G6
Mid Yell	Shet	61	d2
Milborne Port	Somset	7	J1
Mildenhall	Suffk	24	E7
Milfield	Nthumb	47	J6
Milford Haven	Pembks	18	C5
Milford on Sea	Hants	8	D6
Millbrook	Cnwll	3	K5
Millbrook	Jersey	7	b2
Millom	Cumb	36	E5
Millport	N Ayrs	44	F3
Milnathort	P & K	50	F6
Milngavie	E Duns	45	J1
Milton Abbas	Dorset	7	K2
Milton Abbot	Devon	3	K3
Milton Damerel	Devon	4	D6
Milton Ernest	Bed	23	K5
Milton Keynes	M Keyn	23	J6
Milverton	Somset	5	K5
Minchinhampton	Gloucs	13	J2
Minehead	Somset	5	J3
Minster	Kent	11	H2
Minster	Kent	11	L2
Minsterley	Shrops	28	B8
Minster Lovell	Oxon	14	A3
Mintlaw	Abers	61	G4
Mirfield	Kirk	33	K5
Misterton	Notts	34	E7
Misterton	Somset	7	H2
Mitcheldean	Gloucs	21	K7
Mobberley	Ches E	28	E2
Mochrum	D & G	40	E6
Modbury	Devon	3	M5
Moffat	D & G	41	L2
Mold	Flints	27	K4
Moniaive	D & G	41	H3
Monifieth	Angus	51	K4
Monkleigh	Devon	4	D5
Monkton	S Ayrs	45	G5
Monmouth	Mons	21	J8
Montacute	Somset	7	H1
Montford Bridge	Shrops	28	B7
Montgomery	Powys	20	F1
Montrose	Angus	51	L2
Mont Saint	Guern	6	a2
Monyash	Derbys	29	H3
Monymusk	Abers	55	K3
Morchard Bishop	Devon	5	G6
Morcott	Rutlnd	23	J1
Mordiford	Herefs	21	J6
Morebattle	Border	47	H7
Morecambe	Lancs	37	G6
Moreton	Dorset	7	K3
Moretonhampstead	Devon	6	B3
Moreton-in-Marsh	Gloucs	22	C6
Morfa Nefyn	Gwynd	26	B5
Morley	Leeds	33	L4
Morpeth	Nthumb	43	J3
Morston	Norfk	25	G2
Mortehoe	Devon	4	D3
Mortimer	W Berk	14	D7

Morville Shrops............21 K2
Morwenstow Cnwll........4 B3
Mossat Abers...............55 H3
Mosstodloch Moray....59 L4
Mosterton Dorset..........7 H2
Mostyn Flints...............27 K2
Motherby Cumb...........37 G1
Motherwell N Lans......45 K3
Moulsford Oxon...........14 D5
Moulton Nhants...........23 H4
Mountain Ash
    Rhondd..................12 B2
Mountsorrel Leics........30 C7
Mousehole Cnwll...........2 B7
Moy Highld...................58 F5
Muchalls Abers............55 M5
Much Birch Herefs........21 J7
Much Hadham Herts....16 C5
Much Marcle Herefs....21 K2
Much Wenlock
    Shrops....................21 K1
Muddiford Devon...........4 E4
Mulrdrum Angus...........51 K3
Muirhead Angus..........51 H4
Muirkirk E Ayrs............45 K5
Muir of Ord Highld.......58 D4
Muker N York...............37 L4
Mullion Cnwll.................2 D8
Mundesley Norfk..........25 K3
Mundford Norfk...........24 E6
Mungrisdale Cumb........42 B8
Munlochy Highld...........58 E4
Munslow Shrops............21 J2
Musselburgh E Loth....46 D3
Muthill P & K...............50 D5

N

Nacton Suffk................17 K4
Nailsea N Som............12 F4
Nailsworth Gloucs.......13 J2
Nairn Highld................59 G4
Nantgaredig Carmth....19 H4
Nantwich Ches E........28 D5
Narberth Pembks........18 E5
Narborough Norfk.......24 E4
Naseby Nhants...........23 G3
Navenby Lincs............30 F4
Nayland Suffk.............17 H4
Nazeing Essex............16 C6
Neath Neath...............19 K6
Necton Norfk..............24 F5
Needham Market
    Suffk.....................17 J2
Nefyn Gwynd..............26 C5
Nelson Lancs..............33 H3
Nesscliffe Shrops.......28 B7
Neston Ches W...........27 L3
Nether Stowey
    Somset..................12 C7
Nether Wasdale
    Cumb....................36 E3
Nethy Bridge Highld....54 D3
Nettlebed Oxon...........14 E5
Nevern Pembks...........18 E3
Newark-on-Trent
    Notts.....................30 E4
Newarthill N Lans........45 L2
Newbiggin Dur............37 L1
Newbiggin N York........38 A5
Newbiggin-by-the-
    Sea Nthumb...........43 K3
Newbigging S Lans......46 A5
Newbold on Stour
    Warwks.................22 D5
New Bolingbroke
    Lincs.....................31 J4
Newborough IoA.........26 D4
Newbridge Caerph.......12 C2
Newbridge D & G.........41 K4
Newbridge on Wye
    Powys...................20 E4
New Buckenham
    Norfk....................25 H6
Newburgh Abers.........61 G6
Newburgh Fife............51 G5
Newbury W Berk.........14 C6
Newby Bridge Cumb....37 G5
Newcastle Emlyn
    Carmth..................18 F3
Newcastleton Border..42 C3
Newcastle-under-
    Lyme Staffs...........28 F5
Newcastle upon
    Tyne N u Ty...........43 K5
New Cumnock E Ayrs..45 J6

New Deer Abers..........60 F5
Newent Gloucs...........21 L7
Newgale Pembks........18 C4
New Galloway D & G...41 G4
New Grimsby IoS..........2 a1
Newhaven E Susx.......10 C7
New Holland N Linc.....35 G4
Newick E Susx............10 C6
New Luce D & G..........40 C5
Newlyn Cnwll................2 B7
Newmains N Lans........45 L3
Newmarket Suffk.........16 E2
Newmill Moray............60 B4
New Milton Hants..........8 C6
Newnham Gloucs........13 G1
Newnham Worcs.........21 K4
New Pitsligo Abers......60 F4
Newport Essex............16 D4
Newport IoW................8 E6
Newport Newpt..........12 D3
Newport Pembks.........18 D3
Newport Wrekin..........28 E7
Newport-on-Tay Fife...51 J4
Newport Pagnell
    M Keyn..................23 J6
New Quay Cerdgn.......19 G3
Newquay Cnwll.............2 E5
New Radnor Powys......20 F4
New Romney Kent.......11 H5
Newsham N York.........38 B3
Newton Abbot
    Devon.....................6 C5
Newton Aycliffe Dur....38 C2
Newton Ferrers
    Devon.....................3 L6
Newton Ferry W Isls...62 d8
Newtongrange
    Mdloth...................46 D4
Newton Mearns
    E Rens...................45 J3
Newtonmore Highld....54 B4
Newton-on-the-
    Moor Nthumb.........43 J2
Newton on Trent
    Lincs.....................30 E3
Newton St Cyres
    Devon.....................6 C3
Newton Solney
    Derbys...................29 J7
Newton Stewart
    D & G....................40 E5
Newtown Herefs.........21 K5
Newtown Powys.........20 F2
New Tredegar
    Caerph..................12 C2
Newtyle Angus...........51 H3
Neyland Pembks........18 D5
Nigg Highld................59 G3
Ninfield E Susx...........10 E6
Niton IoW....................8 F7
Nocton Lincs..............31 G4
Norham Nthumb.........47 J5
Normanton Wakefd....34 B4
Northall Bucks............15 G2
Northallerton N York...38 D4
Northam Devon............4 D4
Northampton Nhants...23 H4
North Berwick E Loth..46 F2
North Cave E R Yk.......34 F4
Northchapel W Susx.....9 J3
North Chideock
    Dorset....................7 G3
North Cotes Lincs.......35 K4
North Creake Norfk.....24 F3
North Curry Somset...12 D8
North Dalton E R Yk....34 F2
North Elmham Norfk....25 G4
North Ferriby E R Yk...35 G4
North Frodingham
    E R Yk...................35 H2
North Grimston
    N York...................39 H6
North Hayling Hants.....9 G5
North Hykeham
    Lincs.....................30 F3
Northiam E Susx.........11 G6
North Kessock
    Highld...................58 F4
North Kilworth Leics...23 G3
North Kyme Lincs.......31 H4
Northleach Gloucs......22 C8
North Luffenham
    Rutlnd...................23 J1
North Molton Devon.....5 G4
North Muskham
    Notts.....................30 E4
Northop Flints.............27 K3
North Petherton
    Somset..................12 D7
North Rigton N York...33 L2
North Shields N Tyne..43 K5

North Somercotes
    Lincs.....................35 K6
North Walsham Norfk..25 J3
North Waltham Hants....8 F2
North Weald Bassett
    Essex....................16 D6
Northwich Ches W......28 D3
North Wingfield
    Derbys...................29 K4
Northwold Norfk.........24 E6
Norton N York............39 G6
Norton St Philip
    Somset..................13 H5
Norwich Norfk............25 J5
Nottingham C Nott......30 C5
Nuneaton Warwks......22 E2
Nunney Somset..........13 H6
Nutley E Susx............10 C5

O

Oadby Leics...............23 G1
Oakham Rutlnd..........30 E8
Oakhill Somset...........13 G6
Oakley Bed................23 K5
Oakley Bucks.............14 D3
Oakley Hants..............8 F2
Oare Wilts.................13 L5
Oban Ag & B..............52 F7
Ochiltree E Ayrs.........45 H5
Ockbrook Derbys........29 L6
Ockley Surrey..............9 L2
Odiham Hants..............9 G2
Offenham Worcs........22 B5
Ogbourne St George
    Wilts.....................13 M4
Ogmore-by-Sea
    V Glam..................19 L8
Okehampton Devon......4 E7
Old Deer Abers..........61 G4
Old Grimsby IoS...........2 a1
Oldham Oldham..........33 H6
Old Hurst Cambs........24 A7
Old Leake Lincs.........31 K5
Oldmeldrum Abers......60 F6
Old Rayne Abers........60 D6
Old Sodbury S Glos....13 H3
Old Stratford Nhants...23 H6
Old Town IoS...............2 b2
Old Windsor W & M....15 G6
Ollaberry Shet...........61 b3
Ollerton Notts............30 C3
Olney M Keyn............23 J5
Ombersley Worcs......21 M4
Onchan IoM...............36 c3
Onich Highld..............53 G5
Orford Suffk...............17 L3
Ormesby St
    Margaret Norfk......25 L4
Ormskirk Lancs..........32 D6
Orpington Gt Lon.......10 D2
Orsett Thurr..............10 E1
Orton Cumb...............37 J3
Osbournby Lincs........31 G6
Osmington Dorset.......7 K4
Osmotherley N York...38 D4
Ospringe Kent...........11 H3
Ossett Wakefd...........33 L5
Oswaldkirk N York......38 F5
Oswestry Shrops.......27 L6
Otford Kent...............10 D3
Othery Somset...........12 E7
Otley Leeds...............33 K3
Otterbourne Hants.......8 E4
Otterburn Nthumb......43 G3
Otter Ferry Ag & B.....49 H5
Ottershaw Surrey......15 G2
Otterton Devon............6 E4
Ottery St Mary Devon..6 E3
Oundle Nhants...........23 K2
Outwell Norfk............24 C5
Overseal Derbys........29 K7
Overton Hants.............8 F2
Overton Wrexhm.......28 B5
Ower Hants.................8 D4
Oxford Oxon..............14 C3
Oxted Surrey.............10 C3
Oxton Notts...............30 C5
Oxwich Swans...........19 H7

P

Padbury Bucks..........23 H7
Paddock Wood Kent..10 E4
Padiham Lancs..........33 G4
Padstow Cnwll............2 F4
Paignton Torbay.........6 C5

Pailton Warwks..........22 F3
Painswick Gloucs.......13 J1
Paisley Rens..............45 H2
Palnackie D & G.........41 J6
Pandy Mons...............21 G7
Pangbourne W Berk...14 D6
Pannal N York............33 L2
Pant-y-dwr Powys......20 E3
Papworth Everard
    Cambs...................16 B2
Parracombe Devon.......4 F3
Pateley Bridge
    N York...................38 B6
Patna E Ayrs.............45 H6
Patrick IoM................36 b3
Patrington E R Yk.......35 J4
Patterdale Cumb........37 G2
Pattishall Nhants........23 G5
Peacehaven E Susx...10 C7
Peasedown St John
    BaNES....................13 H5
Peasmarsh E Susx.....11 G6
Peebles Border..........46 C5
Peel IoM....................36 b3
Pelynt Cnwll................3 H5
Pembrey Carmth.........19 G6
Pembridge Herefs......21 H4
Pembroke Pembks......18 D6
Pembroke Dock
    Pembks..................18 D6
Pembury Kent............10 E4
Penally Pembks..........18 E6
Penarth V Glam..........12 C4
Pencoed Brdgnd.........12 A3
Pencraig Herefs.........21 J7
Pendine Carmth..........18 F5
Pendock Worcs..........21 L6
Pendoggett Cnwll........3 G3
Pengam Caerph..........12 C2
Penicuik Mdloth.........46 C4
Penistone Barns........33 L6
Penkridge Staffs........29 G7
Penmachno Conwy....27 G5
Penmaenmawr
    Conwy...................26 F3
Pennal Gwynd............20 B1
Pennan Abers............60 F3
Penpont D & G...........41 J3
Penrhyndeudraeth
    Gwynd...................26 E6
Penrith Cumb.............42 D8
Penryn Cnwll...............2 E7
Pensford BaNES.........13 G5
Penshurst Kent..........10 D4
Pensilva Cnwll.............3 J4
Pentewan Cnwll..........2 F6
Pentraeth IoA.............26 D3
Pentrefoelas Conwy...27 G5
Penybont Powys.........20 F4
Pen-y-bont-fawr
    Powys...................27 J7
Penygroes Gwynd......26 D4
Penzance Cnwll...........2 B7
Perranporth Cnwll.......2 D5
Pershore Worcs.........22 A5
Perth P & K................50 F4
Peterborough C Pete..23 M1
Peterchurch Herefs....21 H6
Peterculter C Aber.....55 L4
Peterhead Abers........61 H5
Peterlee Dur..............43 L7
Petersfield Hants.........9 H4
Petton Devon...............5 J5
Petworth W Susx........9 J4
Pevensey E Susx.......10 E7
Pewsey Wilts.............13 L5
Pickering N York........39 G5
Piercebridge Darltn...38 C2
Pierowall Ork.............65 C1
Pillaton Cnwll..............3 J4
Pillerton Priors
    Warwks.................22 D5
Pilling Lancs..............32 D3
Pinchbeck Lincs.........31 H7
Pinwherry S Ayrs.......40 C3
Pinxton Derbys..........29 L4
Pirbright Surrey.........15 G2
Pitcaple Abers...........60 E6
Pitlochry P & K...........50 E2
Pitmedden Abers........60 F6
Pittenweem Fife.........51 K6
Pleasley Derbys.........30 B4
Plockton Highld..........57 H6
Pluckley Kent............11 G4
Plumpton E Susx.......10 C6
Plumtree Notts...........30 C6
Plymouth C Plym.........3 K5
Plympton C Plym.........3 L5
Pocklington E R Yk....34 E2
Polbathic Cnwll...........3 J5
Polegate E Susx........10 D7

Polmont Falk 50 E8
Polperro Cnwll 3 H5
Polruan Cnwll 3 G5
Polzeath Cnwll 2 F3
Pontardawe Neath 19 K6
Pontarddulais Swans 19 J6
Pontefract Wakefd 34 B5
Ponteland Nthumb 43 J4
Ponterwyd Cerdgn 20 C3
Pontesbury Shrops 28 B8
Pontllanfraith Caerph 12 C2
Pontrhydfendigaid Cerdgn 20 K1
Pontrilas Herefs 21 H7
Pontyates Carmth 19 H5
Pontyberem Carmth 19 H5
Pontypool Torfn 12 D2
Pontypridd Rhondd 12 B3
Pool Leeds 33 L3
Poole Poole 8 A6
Poolewe Highld 57 H2
Pooley Bridge Cumb 37 H2
Porlock Somset 5 H3
Porlock Weir Somset 5 H3
Port Appin Ag & B 52 F6
Port Askaig Ag & B 48 D6
Portavadie Ag & B 49 H6
Port Bannatyne Ag & B 49 J6
Port Carlisle Cumb 42 A5
Port Charlotte Ag & B 48 B7
Portchester Hants 8 F5
Port Ellen Ag & B 48 C8
Port Erin IoM 36 a4
Portesham Dorset 7 J3
Port Eynon Swans 19 H7
Port Glasgow Inver 49 L5
Portgordon Moray 60 B3
Porth Rhondd 12 B3
Porthcawl Brdgnd 19 L8
Porthcothan Cnwll 2 E4
Porthcurno Cnwll 2 A8
Port Henderson Highld 57 G3
Porthleven Cnwll 2 C7
Porthmadog Gwynd 26 E6
Porthtowan Cnwll 2 D6
Portinscale Cumb 36 F2
Port Isaac Cnwll 2 F3
Portishead N Som 12 F4
Portknockie Moray 60 C3
Portlethen Abers 55 M5
Portloe Cnwll 2 F6
Port Logan D & G 40 C7
Portmahomack Highld 59 H2
Portnacroish Ag & B 53 G6
Portnahaven Ag & B 48 A7
Port nan Long W Isls 62 d8
Port Nis W Isls 62 i1
Port of Menteith Stirlg 50 B6
Port of Ness W Isls 62 i1
Portpatrick D & G 40 B6
Portreath Cnwll 2 C6
Portree Highld 56 E5
Port St Mary IoM 36 a4
Portscatho Cnwll 2 E7
Portskerra Highld 64 E2
Portslade-by-Sea Br & H 10 B7
Portsmouth C Port 9 G5
Portsoy Abers 60 D3
Port Talbot Neath 19 K7
Port William D & G 40 E7
Postbridge Devon 3 M3
Postcombe Oxon 14 E4
Potterne Wilts 13 K5
Potters Bar Herts 15 J4
Potton C Beds 16 B3
Poulton-le-Fylde Lancs 32 C3
Powburn Nthumb 47 K7
Powick Worcs 21 M5
Poynton Ches E 28 F2
Praa Sands Cnwll 2 C7
Prees Shrops 28 C6
Preesall Lancs 32 C3
Prees Green Shrops 28 C6
Prenteg Gwynd 26 E5
Prestatyn Denbgs 27 J2
Prestbury Ches E 28 F3
Presteigne Powys 21 G4
Preston Border 47 H4
Preston Lancs 32 E4
Preston Candover Hants 8 F2
Preston Capes Nhants 22 F5

Prestonpans E Loth 46 E3
Prestwich Bury 33 G6
Prestwick S Ayrs 45 G5
Priddy Somset 12 F6
Princes Risborough Bucks 14 F4
Princethorpe Warwks .. 22 E3
Princetown Devon 3 L4
Prospect Cumb 41 L7
Prudhoe Nthumb 43 H5
Pucklechurch S Glos .. 13 H4
Puddletown Dorset 7 K3
Pudsey Leeds 33 L4
Pulborough W Susx 9 K4
Pulford Ches W 28 B4
Pulham St Mary Norfk 25 J7
Pumsaint Carmth 19 J3
Purfleet Thurr 10 D1
Purton Wilts 13 L3
Pwll Carmth 19 H6
Pwllheli Gwynd 26 C6
Pyecombe W Susx 10 B6
Pyle Brdgnd 19 L7

Q

Quatt Shrops 21 L2
Queensferry Flints 27 L3
Quendon Essex 16 D4

R

Rackenford Devon 5 H5
Rackheath Norfk 25 J4
Radcliffe on Trent Notts 30 C6
Radlett Herts 15 H4
Radstock BaNES 13 G5
Radwinter Essex 16 E4
Radyr Cardif 12 C4
Rafford Moray 59 J4
Raglan Mons 12 E1
Rainham Gt Lon 10 D1
Rampside Cumb 36 F6
Ramsbury Wilts 14 A6
Ramsey Cambs 24 A7
Ramsey IoM 36 c2
Ramsgate Kent 11 L2
Rannoch Station P & K 53 L5
Rapness Ork 65 c2
Rathen Abers 61 G3
Raunds Nhants 23 K3
Ravenglass Cumb 36 E4
Ravenscar N York 39 J3
Ravenstonedale Cumb 37 K3
Rawmarsh Rothm 34 B7
Rawtenstall Lancs 33 G4
Rayleigh Essex 16 F7
Reading Readg 14 E6
Reay Highld 64 F2
Reculver Kent 11 K2
Redbourn Herts 15 H3
Redbrook Gloucs 12 F1
Redbrook Wrexhm 28 C5
Redcar R & Cl 38 F2
Redditch Worcs 22 B4
Redgrave Suffk 25 G7
Redhill N Som 12 F5
Redhill Surrey 10 B4
Redmile Leics 30 E6
Rednal Shrops 28 B6
Red Roses Carmth 18 F5
Red Row Nthumb 43 K2
Redruth Cnwll 2 D6
Red Wharf Bay IoA 26 D2
Reedham Norfk 25 L5
Reepham Norfk 25 H4
Reigate Surrey 10 B4
Reighton N York 39 K5
Rempstone Notts 30 C7
Renfrew Rens 45 H2
Renwick Cumb 42 D7
Repton Derbys 29 K6
Resolven Neath 19 L6
Retford Notts 30 D2
Reynoldston Swans 19 H7
Rhayader Powys 20 D4
Rhiconich Highld 63 H3
Rhoose V Glam 5 J2
Rhoslanerchrugog Wrexhm 27 L5
Rhosneigr IoA 26 C3
Rhôs-on-Sea Conwy 27 G2
Rhossili Swans 19 G7

Rhu Ag & B 49 L5
Rhuddlan Denbgs 27 J3
Rhyd-Ddu Gwynd 26 E4
Rhydowen Cerdgn 19 G2
Rhyl Denbgs 27 H2
Rhymney Caerph 12 C1
Richards Castle Herefs 21 J4
Richmond Gt Lon 15 J6
Richmond N York 38 B3
Rickmansworth Herts 15 H4
Riding Mill Nthumb 43 H5
Ridsdale Nthumb 43 G4
Rillington N York 39 H5
Ringford D & G 41 G6
Ringmer E Susx 10 C6
Ringwood Hants 8 C5
Ripley Derbys 29 K5
Ripley N York 38 C7
Ripley Surrey 15 H7
Ripon N York 38 D6
Ripple Worcs 21 M6
Rippenden Calder 33 J5
Risca Caerph 12 D3
Risegate Lincs 31 H6
Riseley Bed 23 K4
Riseley Wokham 14 E7
Risley Derbys 29 L6
Risley Warrtn 32 F7
Roade Nhants 23 H5
Roberton Border 46 E7
Roberton S Lans 45 M5
Robertsbridge E Susx 10 F6
Robeston Wathen Pembks 18 E5
Robin Hood's Bay N York 39 J3
Rocester Staffs 29 H6
Roch Pembks 18 C4
Rochdale Rochdl 33 H5
Roche Cnwll 2 F5
Rochester Medway 10 F2
Rochester Nthumb 42 F3
Rochford Essex 17 G7
Rock Cnwll 2 F3
Rockcliffe Cumb 42 B5
Rockcliffe D & G 41 J6
Rockingham Nhants 23 J2
Rogate W Susx 9 H4
Rogerstone Newpt 12 D3
Rollesby Norfk 25 L4
Rolvenden Kent 11 G5
Romaldkirk Dur 37 M2
Romanno Bridge Border 46 C5
Romford Gt Lon 16 D7
Romsey Hants 8 D4
Rookhope Dur 43 G7
Ropley Hants 9 G3
Rosedale Abbey N York 39 G4
Rosehall Highld 63 K7
Rosehearty Abers 61 G3
Rosemarkie Highld 58 F4
Rosewell Mdloth 46 D4
Rossett Wrexhm 28 B4
Ross-on-Wye Herefs .. 21 K7
Rosyth Fife 46 B2
Rothbury Nthumb 43 H2
Rotherfield E Susx 10 D5
Rotherham Rothm 34 B7
Rothes Moray 59 L4
Rothesay Ag & B 49 J6
Rothwell Leeds 33 M4
Rothwell Nhants 23 J3
Rottingdean Br & H 10 C7
Roughton Norfk 25 J3
Rowland's Castle Hants 9 G5
Rowland's Gill Gatesd . 43 J6
Rowsley Derbys 29 J3
Roxburgh Border 47 G6
Roxwell Essex 16 E6
Royal Leamington Spa Warwks 22 D4
Royal Tunbridge Wells Kent 10 E4
Royal Wootton Bassett Wilts 13 L3
Royston Barns 34 A5
Royston Herts 16 C4
Rozel Jersey 7 c1
Ruabon Wrexhm 27 L5
Ruddington Notts 30 C6
Rudgwick W Susx 9 K3
Rudston E R Yk 39 K6
Rufford Lancs 32 D5
Rugby Warwks 22 F3
Rugeley Staffs 29 G7

Rumbling Bridge P & K 50 F6
Runcorn Halton 28 C2
Rushden Nhants 23 K4
Rushyford Dur 38 C1
Ruskington Lincs 31 G5
Rustington W Susx 9 K5
Ruswarp N York 39 H3
Rutherglen S Lans 45 J2
Ruthin Denbgs 27 J4
Ruyton-XI-Towns Shrops 28 B7
Rydal Cumb 37 G3
Ryde IoW 8 F6
Rye E Susx 11 G6

S

Saddell Ag & B 44 B5
Saffron Walden Essex 16 D4
St Abbs Border 47 J3
St Agnes Cnwll 2 D5
St Albans Herts 15 H3
St Andrew Guern 6 a2
St Andrews Fife 51 K5
St Arvans Mons 12 F2
St Asaph Denbgs 27 J3
St Athan V Glam 5 J1
St Aubin Jersey 7 b2
St Austell Cnwll 2 F5
St Bees Cumb 36 D3
St Blazey Cnwll 3 G5
St Boswells Border 46 F6
St Brelade Jersey 7 a2
St Brelade's Bay Jersey 7 a2
St Briavels Gloucs 12 F2
St Buryan Cnwll 2 A7
St Catherines Ag & B .. 49 J3
St Clears Carmth 18 F5
St Cleer Cnwll 3 H4
St Clement Jersey 7 c1
St Columb Major Cnwll 2 F4
St Combs Abers 61 H3
St Cyrus Abers 55 K7
St David's Pembks 18 B4
St Day Cnwll 2 D6
St Dogmaels Pembks .. 18 E2
St Fergus Abers 61 H4
St Fillans P & K 50 C4
St Florence Pembks 18 E6
St Helens IoW 9 G6
St Helens St Hel 32 E7
St Helier Jersey 7 b2
St Ives Cambs 24 A8
St Ives Cnwll 2 B6
St John Jersey 7 b1
St John's IoM 36 b3
St John's Chapel Dur .. 43 G7
St John's Town of Dalry D & G 41 G4
St Jude's IoM 36 c2
St Just Cnwll 2 A7
St Just-in-Roseland Cnwll 2 E7
St Keverne Cnwll 2 E8
St Keyne Cnwll 3 H5
St Lawrence IoW 8 F7
St Lawrence Jersey 7 b1
St Margaret's at Cliffe Kent 11 L4
St Margaret's Hope Ork 65 c5
St Marks IoM 36 b3
St Martin Guern 6 a2
St Martin Jersey 7 c1
St Mary Jersey 7 b1
St Mary's Ork 65 c4
St Mary's Bay Kent 11 J3
St Mawes Cnwll 2 E7
St Mawgan Cnwll 2 E4
St Monans Fife 51 K6
St Neots Cambs 23 M4
St Osyth Essex 17 J5
St Ouen Jersey 7 a1
St Owens Cross Herefs 21 J7
St Peter Jersey 7 b1
St Peter Port Guern 6 b2
St Peter's Guern 6 a2
St Sampson Guern 6 b2
St Saviour Guern 6 a2
St Saviour Jersey 7 b2
St Stephen Cnwll 2 F5
St Tudy Cnwll 3 G3
Salcombe Devon 6 B7
Sale Traffd 33 G7

Salen Ag & B.............52 D6
Salen Highld.............52 E4
Salfords Surrey..........10 B4
Saline Fife..............50 F7
Salisbury Wilts...........8 C3
Saltash Cnwll.............3 K5
Saltburn-by-the-Sea
   R & Cl................38 F2
Saltcoats N Ayrs.........44 F4
Saltfleet Lincs..........35 K7
Sampford Arundel
   Somset................5 K5
Sampford Brett
   Somset................5 J3
Sanaigmore Ag & B.......48 B6
Sandbach Ches E.........28 E4
Sandbank Ag & B.........49 K5
Sandford-on-
   Thames Oxon..........14 C4
Sandhaven Abers.........61 G3
Sandhead D & G..........40 C6
Sandhurst Br For........14 F7
Sandness Shet...........61 a5
Sandon Staffs...........29 G6
Sandown IoW..............8 F7
Sandridge Herts.........15 J3
Sandsend N York.........39 H3
Sandwich Kent...........11 L3
Sandwick Shet...........61 c7
Sandy C Beds............23 L5
Sanquhar D & G..........45 L6
Sarn Gwynd..............26 B6
Sarre Kent..............11 K2
Saundby Notts...........34 E7
Saundersfoot
   Pembks...............18 E5
Saunton Devon............4 D4
Sawbridgeworth
   Herts................16 D5
Sawston Cambs...........16 D3
Sawtry Cambs............23 L3
Saxby Leics.............30 E7
Saxilby Lincs...........30 E3
Saxmundham Suffk........17 L2
Saxthorpe Norfk.........25 H3
Scalasaig Ag & B........48 C4
Scalby N York...........39 J4
Scalloway Shet..........61 c6
Scamblesby Lincs........31 J3
Scarborough N York......39 K4
Scarinish Ag & B........48 b2
Scawby N Linc...........34 F6
Scole Norfk.............25 H7
Scone P & K.............51 G4
Sconser Highld..........56 E6
Scotch Corner N York....38 C3
Scotter Lincs...........34 F6
Scotton N York..........38 B4
Scoulton Norfk..........25 G5
Scourie Highld..........63 G4
Scrabster Highld........65 G2
Scunthorpe N Linc.......34 F5
Seaford E Susx..........10 D7
Seaham Dur..............43 L6
Seahouses Nthumb........47 L6
Seal Kent...............10 D3
Seamer N York...........39 J4
Sea Palling Norfk.......25 L3
Seascale Cumb...........36 D3
Seathwaite Cumb.........36 F4
Seaton Devon.............6 F3
Seaton Delaval
   Nthumb...............43 K4
Seave Green N York......38 D2
Seaview IoW..............9 G6
Sedbergh Cumb...........37 J4
Sedgeberrow Worcs.......22 B6
Sedgebrook Lincs........30 E6
Sedgefield Dur..........38 D1
Sedlescombe E Susx......10 F6
Seend Wilts.............13 K5
Selborne Hants...........9 G3
Selby N York............34 B4
Selkirk Border..........46 E6
Sellindge Kent..........11 J4
Selsey W Susx............9 H6
Selston Notts...........29 L4
Send Surrey.............15 G7
Sennen Cnwll.............2 A7
Sennybridge Powys.......20 D4
Setchey Norfk...........24 D4
Settle N York...........37 L6
Sevenoaks Kent..........10 D3
Seven Sisters Neath.....19 L5
Shaftesbury Dorset......13 J8
Shalford Essex..........16 F4
Shalford Surrey..........9 K2
Shandon Ag & B..........49 J6
Shanklin IoW.............8 F7
Shap Cumb...............37 H2
Shardlow Derbys.........29 L6

Sharnbrook Bed..........23 K4
Sharpness Gloucs........13 G2
Shaugh Prior Devon.......3 L4
Shavington Ches E.......28 E5
Shawbury Shrops.........28 C7
Shebbear Devon...........4 D6
Sheepwash Devon..........4 E6
Sheerness Kent..........11 G2
Sheffield Sheff.........29 K2
Shefford C Beds.........23 L6
Shepreth Cambs..........16 C3
Shepshed Leics..........30 B7
Shepton Mallet
   Somset...............13 G6
Sherborne Dorset.........7 J1
Sherburn N York.........39 J5
Sherburn in Elmet
   N York...............34 C4
Sherfield on Loddon
   Hants................14 D7
Sheriff Hutton
   N York...............38 F6
Sheringham Norfk........25 H2
Shiel Bridge Highld.....57 J7
Shieldaig Highld........57 H4
Shifnal Shrops..........28 E8
Shildon Dur.............38 C2
Shillingford Oxon.......14 D4
Shillingstone Dorset.....7 L2
Shinfield Wokham........14 E6
Shinness Highld.........63 K6
Shipdham Norfk..........25 G5
Shiplake Oxon...........14 E6
Shipley C Brad..........33 K3
Shipston on Stour
   Warwks...............22 D6
Shipton N York..........38 E7
Shiptonthorpe E R Yk....34 E3
Shirebrook Derbys.......30 B3
Shoreham-by-Sea
   W Susx................9 L5
Shorwell IoW.............8 E7
Shotley Suffk...........17 K4
Shottisham Suffk........17 L3
Shotts N Lans...........45 L2
Shrewsbury Shrops.......28 C8
Shrewton Wilts..........13 L6
Shrivenham Oxon.........13 M3
Shurdington Gloucs......22 A7
Shute Devon..............6 F3
Sibsey Lincs............31 J5
Sibson Leics............22 E1
Sidmouth Devon...........6 E3
Silchester Hants........14 D7
Sileby Leics............30 C7
Silk Willoughby Lincs...31 G5
Silloth Cumb............41 L6
Silsoe C Beds...........23 L6
Silverdale Lancs........37 H5
Silver End Essex........16 F5
Silverstone Nhants......23 G6
Silverton Devon..........5 H6
Simonburn Nthumb........42 F4
Simonsbath Somset........5 G4
Singleton W Susx.........9 J4
Sissinghurst Kent.......10 F4
Sittingbourne Kent......11 G3
Sixpenny Handley
   Dorset................8 A4
Skegness Lincs..........31 L4
Skellingthorpe Lincs....30 F3
Skelmersdale Lancs......32 D6
Skelmorlie N Ayrs.......49 K6
Skelton Cumb............42 C7
Skelton R & Cl..........38 F2
Skenfrith Mons..........21 H7
Skerray Highld..........64 C2
Skipness Ag & B.........44 C3
Skipsea E R Yk..........35 H2
Skipton N York..........33 J2
Skirling Border.........46 B6
Skirwith Cumb...........42 D8
Slaidburn Lancs.........32 F2
Slaley Nthumb...........43 G6
Slamannan Falk..........45 L1
Slapton Devon............6 B7
Sleaford Lincs..........31 H4
Sledmere E R Yk.........39 J6
Sleights N York.........39 H3
Slingsby N York.........39 G5
Slough Slough...........15 G5
Smailholm Border........47 G6
Smarden Kent............11 G4
Smithfield Cumb.........42 C5
Snainton N York.........39 J5
Snape Suffk.............17 L2
Snettisham Norfk........24 E3
Snodland Kent...........10 E3
Soham Cambs.............24 D7
Solihull Solhll.........22 C3
Solva Pembks............18 B4

Somersham Cambs.........24 B7
Somerton Somset.........12 F7
Sompting W Susx..........9 L5
Sonning Wokham..........14 E6
Sonning Common
   Oxon.................14 E5
Sorbie D & G............40 E6
Soulby Cumb.............37 K3
Souldern Oxon...........22 F6
Souldrop Bed............23 K4
Sourton Devon............3 L2
Southam Warwks..........22 E4
Southampton C Sotn.......8 E5
South Benfleet Essex....16 F8
Southborough Kent.......10 D4
South Brent Devon........6 A5
South Cave E R Yk.......34 F4
South Elmsall Wakefd....34 B5
Southend Ag & B.........44 B6
Southend-on-Sea
   Sthend...............17 G8
Southery Norfk..........24 D6
South Harting
   W Susx................9 H4
South Hayling Hants......9 G5
South Holmwood
   Surrey................9 L2
South Kyme Lincs........31 H5
South Mimms Herts.......15 J4
Southminster Essex......17 H7
South Molton Devon.......4 F5
Southmoor Oxon..........14 B4
South Normanton
   Derbys...............29 L4
South Ockendon
   Thurr................16 E8
South Petherton
   Somset................7 G1
Southport Sefton........32 C5
South Queensferry
   C Edin...............46 B3
South Raynham
   Norfk................24 F4
Southrepps Norfk........25 J3
Southsea C Port..........9 G6
South Shields S Tyne....43 L5
South Stainley
   N York...............38 C6
South Walsham
   Norfk................25 K4
Southwell Notts.........30 D4
Southwick Hants..........9 G5
Southwick W Susx........10 B7
South Witham Lincs......30 F7
Southwold Suffk.........25 L7
South Woodham
   Ferrers Essex........16 F7
South Zeal Devon.........3 M2
Sowerby N York..........38 D5
Sowerby Bridge
   Calder...............33 J4
Spalding Lincs..........31 H7
Sparkford Somset........13 G8
Sparsholt Hants..........8 E3
Spean Bridge Highld.....53 J3
Spennymoor Dur..........43 K7
Spetisbury Dorset........7 L2
Spey Bay Moray..........60 B3
Spilsby Lincs...........31 K3
Spinningdale Highld.....58 F1
Spittal Highld..........65 H3
Spittal of Glenshee
   P & K................54 E7
Spixworth Norfk.........25 J4
Spofforth N York........34 A2
Springholm D & G........41 H5
Sproatley E R Yk........35 H4
Stadhampton Oxon........14 D4
Stadhlaigearraidh
   W Isls...............62 c11
Staffin Highld..........56 E3
Stafford Staffs.........28 F7
Staindrop Dur...........38 B2
Staines-upon-
   Thames Surrey........15 G6
Stainforth N York.......37 L6
Staithes N York.........39 G2
Stalham Norfk...........25 K4
Stamford Lincs..........31 G8
Stamford Bridge
   E R Yk...............39 G7
Stamfordham
   Nthumb...............43 H5
Standingstone Cumb......41 K7
Standish Wigan..........32 E5
Standon Herts...........16 C5
Stanford in the Vale
   Oxon.................14 B4
Stanford le Hope
   Thurr................16 E1
Stanhope Dur............43 G7

Stanley Dur.............43 J6
Stanley P & K...........50 F4
Stannington Nthumb......43 J4
Stansted
   Mountfitchet
   Essex................16 D5
Stanton Suffk...........25 G7
Stanton St Quintin
   Wilts................13 J4
Stanway Gloucs..........22 B6
Staple Fitzpaine
   Somset................6 F1
Stapleford Notts........30 B6
Staplehurst Kent........10 F4
Starbotton N York.......37 M5
Staveley Cumb...........37 H4
Staveley Derbys.........29 L3
Staverton Nhants........22 F4
Staxton N York..........39 J5
Steeple Essex...........17 G6
Steeple Aston Oxon......22 F7
Steeple Bumpstead
   Essex................16 E3
Stenhousemuir Falk......50 D8
Steornabhagh W Isls.....62 h3
Stevenage Herts.........16 B5
Stevenston N Ayrs.......44 F4
Steventon Oxon..........14 C5
Stewarton E Ayrs........45 H3
Stewkley Bucks..........23 J7
Steyning W Susx..........9 L5
Stibb Cross Devon........4 D5
Stickford Lincs.........31 J4
Stickney Lincs..........31 J4
Stiffkey Norfk..........25 G2
Stilligarry W Isls......62 c11
Stillington N York......38 F6
Stilton Cambs...........23 L2
Stirling Stirlg.........50 D7
Stock Essex.............16 E7
Stockbridge Hants........8 D3
Stockport Stockp........33 H7
Stocksbridge Sheff......33 L6
Stockton-on-Tees
   S on T...............38 E2
Stogursey Somset........12 C6
Stoke by Clare Suffk....16 F3
Stoke-by-Nayland
   Suffk................17 H4
Stoke Canon Devon........6 C3
Stoke Ferry Norfk.......24 E5
Stoke Fleming Devon......6 C6
Stoke Gabriel Devon......6 C6
Stoke Goldington
   M Keyn...............23 J5
Stoke Lacy Herefs.......21 K5
Stoke Mandeville
   Bucks................14 F3
Stokenchurch Bucks......14 E4
Stoke-on-Trent
   C Stke...............28 F5
Stoke Poges Bucks.......15 G5
Stokesley N York........38 E3
Stone Staffs............28 F6
Stonehaven Abers........55 L5
Stonehouse Gloucs.......13 H2
Stonehouse S Lans.......45 K3
Stoneykirk D & G........40 B6
Stonor Oxon.............14 E5
Stornoway W Isls........62 h3
Storrington W Susx.......9 K4
Stotfold C Beds.........16 A4
Stoulton Worcs..........22 A5
Stourbridge Dudley......21 M3
Stourpaine Dorset........7 L2
Stourport-on-
   Severn Worcs.........21 L3
Stourton Staffs.........21 M2
Stow Border.............46 E5
Stow-cum-Quy
   Cambs................16 D2
Stowmarket Suffk........17 H2
Stow-on-the-Wold
   Gloucs...............22 C7
Strachan Abers..........55 K5
Strachur Ag & B.........49 J3
Stradbroke Suffk........25 J7
Stradishall Suffk.......16 F3
Stradsett Norfk.........24 D5
Straiton S Ayrs.........45 G7
Stranraer D & G.........40 B5
Stratfield Turgis
   Hants................14 E7
Stratford St Andrew
   Suffk................17 L2
Stratford-upon-
   Avon Warwks..........22 C5
Strathaven S Lans.......45 K4
Strathblane Stirlg......50 B8
Strathcanaird Highld....63 G7
Strathdon Abers.........55 G3

Strathpeffer Highld 58 D4
Strathy Highld 64 E2
Strathyre Stirlg 50 B5
Stratton Cnwll 4 B6
Stratton-on-the-
  Fosse Somset 13 G6
Streatley W Berk 14 D5
Street Somset 12 F7
Strensall C York 38 F7
Strete Devon 6 C6
Stretford Traffd 33 G7
Stretham Cambs 24 C7
Stretton Rutlnd 30 F7
Strichen Abers 61 G4
Stromeferry Highld 57 H5
Stromness Ork 65 D4
Stronachlachar
  Stirlg 49 M3
Strone Ag & B 49 K5
Strontian Highld 52 F5
Strood Medway 10 F2
Stroud Gloucs 13 J2
Struy Highld 58 C5
Stuartfield Abers 61 G5
Studland Dorset 8 B7
Studley Warwks 22 B4
Sturminster Newton
  Dorset 7 K1
Sturry Kent 11 J3
Sturton by Stow
  Lincs 30 E2
Sudbury Derbys 29 H6
Sudbury Suffk 17 G3
Sulby IoM 36 c2
Summercourt Cnwll 2 E5
Sunbury Surrey 15 H6
Sunderland Sundld 43 L6
Surfleet Lincs 31 H6
Sutterton Lincs 31 J6
Sutton Cambs 24 C7
Sutton Gt Lon 10 B2
Sutton Benger Wilts 13 K4
Sutton Bridge Lincs 24 C4
Sutton Coldfield
  Birm 22 C2
Sutton Courtenay
  Oxon 14 C4
Sutton on Sea Lincs 31 L2
Sutton-on-the-
  Forest N York 38 F6
Sutton on Trent
  Notts 30 E3
Sutton Scotney
  Hants 8 E2
Sutton Valence Kent 10 F4
Swadlincote Derbys 29 K7
Swaffham Norfk 24 F5
Swainswick BaNES 13 H4
Swalcliffe Oxon 22 E6
Swallow Lincs 35 H6
Swallowfield
  Wokham 14 E7
Swanage Dorset 8 B7
Swanley Kent 10 D2
Swansea Swans 19 J6
Swanwick Derbys 29 K4
Swanwick Hants 8 F5
Swaton Lincs 31 G6
Swavesey Cambs 16 C1
Sway Hants 8 D6
Swindon Swindn 13 L3
Swineshead Bed 23 K4
Swineshead Lincs 31 H5
Swinford Leics 22 F3
Swinton Border 47 H5
Swinton Rothm 34 B6
Syderstone Norfk 24 F3
Symbister Shet 61 d4
Symington S Ayrs 45 G5
Symington S Lans 46 A6
Symonds Yat Herefs 21 J8
Syresham Nhants 23 G6
Syston Leics 30 C8

T

Tadcaster N York 34 B3
Tadley Hants 14 D7
Tain Highld 59 G2
Tairbeart W Isls 62 f6
Talgarreg Cerdgn 19 G2
Talgarth Powys 20 F6
Talladale Highld 57 J3
Talley Carmth 19 J3
Talmine Highld 64 C2
Talsarnau Gwynd 26 E6
Tal-y-bont Cerdgn 20 B2
Tal-y-Bont Conwy 26 F3
Tal-y-bont Gwynd 26 E7

Tal-y-Cafn Conwy 27 G3
Tamworth Staffs 22 C1
Tannadice Angus 51 J2
Tan-y-groes Cerdgn 18 F2
Taplow Bucks 14 F5
Tarbert Ag & B 49 G6
Tarbert W Isls 62 f6
Tarbet Ag & B 49 L3
Tarbolton S Ayrs 45 H5
Tarland Abers 55 H4
Tarleton Lancs 32 D5
Tarporley Ches W 28 C4
Tarrant Hinton
  Dorset 7 M2
Tarskavaig Highld 56 F7
Tarves Abers 60 F6
Tarvin Ches W 28 C3
Tattershall Lincs 31 H4
Taunton Somset 12 D8
Taverham Norfk 25 H4
Tavistock Devon 3 K4
Tayinloan Ag & B 44 B3
Taynton Oxon 22 D8
Taynuilt Ag & B 53 G7
Tayport Fife 51 J4
Tayvallich Ag & B 48 F5
Tebay Cumb 37 J3
Tedburn St Mary
  Devon 6 B3
Teddington Gloucs 22 A6
Teignmouth Devon 6 C4
Telford Wrekin 28 E8
Temple Mdloth 46 D4
Temple Bar Cerdgn 19 H2
Templecombe
  Somset 13 H8
Temple Sowerby
  Cumb 37 J1
Tempsford C Beds 23 L5
Tenbury Wells Worcs 21 K4
Tenby Pembks 18 E6
Tenterden Kent 11 G5
Ternhill Shrops 28 D6
Terrington St
  Clement Norfk 24 C4
Tetbury Gloucs 13 J3
Tetford Lincs 31 J3
Tetney Lincs 35 J6
Tetsworth Oxon 14 E4
Teviothead Border 42 C2
Tewkesbury Gloucs 21 M6
Teynham Kent 11 H3
Thame Oxon 14 E4
Thatcham W Berk 14 C6
Thaxted Essex 16 E4
Theale W Berk 14 D6
Theberton Suffk 17 M2
The Bungalow IoM 36 c2
Thetford Norfk 24 F7
Theydon Bois Essex 16 C7
Thirsk N York 38 D5
Thornbury S Glos 13 G3
Thorne Donc 34 D5
Thorney C Pete 24 A5
Thornham Norfk 24 E2
Thornhill D & G 41 J3
Thornhill Stirlg 50 C6
Thornley Dur 43 L7
Thornton Fife 51 H6
Thornton le Dale
  N York 39 H5
Thornton-le-Street
  N York 38 D5
Thornton Watlass
  N York 38 C5
Thorpe End North 25 J3
Thorpe-le-Soken
  Essex 17 J5
Thorpeness Suffk 17 M2
Thorrington Essex 17 J5
Thrapston Nhants 23 K3
Three Cocks Powys 20 F6
Threekingham Lincs 31 G6
Threlkeld Cumb 36 F2
Threshfield N York 37 M6
Thropton Nthumb 43 H2
Thrumster Highld 65 J4
Thurcroft Rothm 34 C7
Thurlestone Devon 6 A7
Thurnscoe Barns 34 B6
Thursby Cumb 42 B6
Thurso Highld 65 G2
Thurstaston Wirral 27 K2
Thurston Suffk 17 G2
Thwaite N York 37 L4
Tibshelf Derbys 29 L4
Ticehurst E Susx 10 E5
Tickhill Donc 34 C7
Ticknall Derbys 29 K7
Tideswell Derbys 29 H3
Tidworth Wilts 8 C2

Tigh a Ghearraidh
  W Isls 62 c8
Tigharry W Isls 62 c8
Tilbury Thurr 10 E2
Tilford Surrey 9 J2
Tillicoultry Clacks 50 E6
Tilshead Wilts 13 K6
Tilstock Shrops 28 C6
Tilton on the Hill
  Leics 30 D8
Tintagel Cnwll 3 G3
Tintern Parva Mons 12 F2
Tiptree Essex 17 G5
Tisbury Wilts 13 K7
Tissington Derbys 29 J5
Tittensor Staffs 28 F6
Tiverton Devon 5 H6
Tobermory Ag & B 52 C5
Toddington C Beds 23 K7
Todmorden Calder 33 H4
Toft Shet 61 c3
Toft Hill Dur 38 B1
Tolastadh W Isls 62 i2
Tollard Royal Wilts 7 M1
Tollesbury Essex 17 H6
Tolleshunt D'Arcy
  Essex 17 G6
Tolpuddle Dorset 7 K3
Tolsta W Isls 62 i2
Tomatin Highld 59 G6
Tomintoul Moray 54 F3
Tomnavoulin Moray 59 K6
Tonbridge Kent 10 E4
Tongue Highld 64 C3
Tonypandy Rhondd 12 B3
Tonyrefail Rhondd 12 B3
Topcliffe N York 38 D5
Topsham Devon 6 D3
Torbeg N Ayrs 44 C5
Torcross Devon 6 B7
Tore Highld 58 E4
Torksey Lincs 30 E3
Torphichen W Loth 46 A3
Torphins Abers 55 J4
Torpoint Cnwll 3 K5
Torquay Torbay 6 C5
Torrance E Duns 45 J1
Torridon Highld 57 H4
Torrin Highld 56 F7
Torryburn Fife 46 B2
Torthorwald D & G 41 K4
Torver Cumb 36 F4
Totland IoW 8 D6
Totnes Devon 6 B5
Totton Hants 8 D4
Towcester Nhants 23 G5
Tow Law Dur 43 J7
Town Yetholm
  Border 47 H6
Traquair Border 46 D6
Trawden Lancs 33 H3
Trawsfynydd Gwynd 26 F6
Trearddur Bay IoA 26 B2
Trecastle Powys 20 D7
Tredegar Blae G 12 C1
Treen Cnwll 2 A8
Trefriw Conwy 27 G4
Tregaron Cerdgn 19 J1
Tregony Cnwll 2 F6
Treherbert Rhondd 19 M6
Trellech Mons 12 F2
Tremadog Gwynd 26 E5
Trimdon Dur 43 L7
Trimingham Norfk 25 J3
Tring Herts 14 F3
Trinity Jersey 7 b1
Troon S Ayrs 45 G5
Trotton W Susx 9 H4
Troutbeck Cumb 37 G3
Trowbridge Wilts 13 J5
Truro Cnwll 2 E6
Tugby Leics 23 H1
Tullibody Clacks 50 D7
Tummel Bridge P & K .. 50 D2
Tunbridge Wells Kent .. 10 E4
Tunstall Suffk 17 L2
Turnberry S Ayrs 44 F7
Turnditch Derbys 29 K5
Turner's Hill W Susx 10 B5
Turriff Abers 60 E4
Turvey Bed 23 K5
Tutbury Staffs 29 J6
Tuxford Notts 30 D3
Twycross Leics 22 E1
Twyford Hants 8 E4
Twyford Wokham 14 E6
Twynholm D & G 41 G6
Tyndrum Stirlg 53 K7
Tynemouth N Tyne 43 L5
Tytherleigh Devon 6 F2
Tywyn Gwynd 20 A1

U

Uckfield E Susx 10 D6
Uffculme Devon 5 J6
Uffington Oxon 14 A5
Ugborough Devon 6 A6
Uig Highld 56 D3
Ulceby N Linc 35 H5
Uldale Cumb 42 A7
Ullapool Highld 63 G7
Ullenhall Warwks 22 C4
Ulpha Cumb 36 E4
Ulsta Shet 61 c3
Ulverston Cumb 36 F5
Umberleigh Devon 4 F5
Unapool Highld 63 H4
Upavon Wilts 13 L5
Uplyme Devon 6 F3
Upottery Devon 6 E2
Upper Beeding
  W Susx 9 L5
Upper Benefield
  Nhants 23 K2
Upper Broughton
  Notts 30 D7
Upper Largo Fife 51 J6
Upper Lydbrook
  Gloucs 21 K8
Upper Tean Staffs 29 G5
Uppingham Rutlnd 23 J1
Upstreet Kent 11 K3
Upton Snodsbury
  Worcs 22 A5
Upton upon Severn
  Worcs 21 M6
Urchfont Wilts 13 K5
Usk Mons 12 E2
Uttoxeter Staffs 29 H6
Uxbridge Gt Lon 15 H5
Uyeasound Shet 61 d2

V

Vale Guern 6 b1
Ventnor IoW 8 F7
Verwood Dorset 8 B5
Vidlin Shet 61 c4
Virginia Water Surrey .. 15 G6
Voe Shet 61 c4

W

Waddesdon Bucks 14 E3
Waddington Lancs 33 G3
Waddington Lincs 30 F4
Wadebridge Cnwll 2 F4
Wadesmill Herts 15 K3
Wadhurst E Susx 10 E5
Wainfleet All Saints
  Lincs 31 K4
Wakefield Wakefd 33 M5
Walberswick Suffk 25 L7
Walgherton Ches E 28 E5
Walkerburn Border 46 D6
Walkern Herts 16 B5
Walkington E R Yk 35 G3
Wallasey Wirral 32 C7
Wallingford Oxon 14 D5
Walls Shet 61 b5
Walsall Wsall 22 B1
Waltham NE Lin 35 J6
Waltham Abbey
  Essex 16 C7
Waltham on the
  Wolds Leics 30 E7
Walton Powys 21 G4
Walton Somset 12 F7
Walton-on-Thames
  Surrey 15 H6
Walton on the Naze
  Essex 17 K5
Wanlockhead D & G 45 L6
Wansford C Pete 23 L1
Wanstrow Somset 13 H6
Wantage Oxon 14 B5
Warboys Cambs 24 A7
Warcop Cumb 37 K2
Wardlow Derbys 29 J3
Ware Herts 15 K3
Wareham Dorset 7 L3
Warenford Nthumb 47 L6
Wargrave Wokham 14 E6
Wark Nthumb 42 F4
Wark Nthumb 47 H6
Warkworth Nthumb 43 K2
Warmington Warwks ... 21 G5

Warminster Wilts 13 J6
Warninglid W Susx 10 B5
Warrington Warrtn 32 F7
Warsash Hants 8 E5
Warslow Staffs 29 H4
Warton Lancs 32 D4
Warwick Warwks 22 D4
Wasbister Ork 65 b2
Wasdale Head Cumb 36 E3
Washingborough
  Lincs 30 F3
Washington Sundld 43 K6
Watchet Somset 5 J3
Watchgate Cumb 37 H4
Waterbeach Cambs 16 D2
Waterbeck D & G 42 A4
Waterhouses Staffs 29 H5
Waterlooville Hants 9 G5
Watermillock Cumb 37 G2
Watford Herts 15 H4
Watford Nhants 23 G4
Wath upon Dearne
  Rothm 34 B6
Watlington Oxon 14 E4
Watten Highld 65 H3
Watton Norfk 24 F5
Watton-at-Stone
  Herts 15 K2
Wearhead Dur 42 F7
Weasenham All
  Saints Norfk 24 F4
Weaverham Ches W 28 D3
Wedmore Somset 12 E6
Weedon Nhants 23 G4
Week St Mary Cnwll 4 B7
Weem P & K 50 D2
Welbourn Lincs 30 F4
Wellesbourne
  Warwks 22 D5
Wellingborough
  Nhants 23 J4
Wellington Somset 5 K5
Wellington Wrekin 28 D8
Wells Somset 12 F6
Wells-next-the-sea
  Norfk 24 F2
Welney Norfk 24 C6
Welshampton Shrops 28 B6
Welshpool Powys 27 K8
Welton Nhants 23 G4
Welwyn Herts 15 J3
Welwyn Garden City
  Herts 15 J3
Wem Shrops 28 C6
Wembley Gt Lon 15 J5
Wembury Devon 3 L6
Wendover Bucks 14 F3
Wensley N York 38 B4
Wentbridge Wakefd 34 B5
Weobley Herefs 21 H5
Wereham Norfk 24 D5
West Auckland Dur 38 B2
West Bay Dorset 7 H3
West Bexington
  Dorset 7 H3
West Bilney Norfk 24 E4
West Bridgford
  Notts 30 C6
West Bromwich
  Sandw 22 B2
Westbury Shrops 28 B8
Westbury Wilts 13 J6
West Calder W Loth 46 A4
West Chiltington
  W Susx 9 K4
Westcott Surrey 9 L2
Westerham Kent 10 C3
West Felton Shrops 27 L7
Westfield E Susx 10 F6
West Haddon Nhants 23 G3
West Hoathly W Susx 10 C5
West Horsley Surrey 15 H8
West Huntspill
  Somset 12 D6
West Kilbride N Ayrs 44 F3
West Kirby Wirral 27 K2
West Lavington Wilts 13 K6
West Linton Border 46 C5
West Lulworth
  Dorset 7 L4
West Lynn Norfk 24 D4
West Malling Kent 10 E3
West Malvern Worcs 21 L5
West Meon Hants 9 G4
West Mersea Essex 17 H6
West Moors Dorset 8 B5
Westnewton Cumb 41 L7
West Newton Norfk 24 E3
Weston Herts 16 B4
Weston Staffs 29 G6
Westonbirt Gloucs 13 J3
Weston Heath
  Shrops 28 E7
Weston-on-the-
  Green Oxon 14 C3
Weston-sub-Edge
  Gloucs 22 C6
Weston-super-Mare
  N Som 12 D5
Weston-under-
  Redcastle Shrops 28 D6
West Pennard
  Somset 12 F7
West Pentire Cnwll 2 D5
West Rounton N York 38 D3
West Runton Norfk 25 J2
Westruther Border 47 G5
West Sandwick Shet 61 C3
Westward Ho! Devon 4 D4
West Wittering
  W Susx 9 H6
West Witton N York 38 A4
West Woodburn
  Nthumb 43 G3
Wetheral Cumb 42 C6
Wetherby Leeds 34 B3
Wetwang E R Yk 39 J7
Weybourne Norfk 25 H2
Weybridge Surrey 15 H7
Weyhill Hants 8 D2
Weymouth Dorset 7 J4
Whaley Bridge
  Derbys 29 G2
Whalley Lancs 33 G3
Whaplode Lincs 31 J7
Whaplode Drove
  Lincs 31 J7
Whauphill D & G 40 E6
Wheathampstead
  Herts 15 J3
Wheatley Oxon 14 D3
Wheddon Cross
  Somset 5 H4
Whepstead Suffk 17 G2
Wherwell Hants 8 E2
Whickham Gatesd 43 J5
Whiddon Down
  Devon 6 A3
Whimple Devon 6 D3
Whipsnade C Beds 15 G3
Whitburn W Loth 46 A4
Whitby N York 39 H3
Whitchurch Bucks 14 E2
Whitchurch Hants 8 E2
Whitchurch Herefs 21 J8
Whitchurch Shrops 28 C5
Whitebridge Highld 58 D7
Whitehaven Cumb 36 D2
Whitehill and
  Bordon Hants 9 H3
Whitehills Abers 60 D3
Whitehouse Ag & B 49 G6
Whitekirk E Loth 46 F2
Whitewell Lancs 32 F3
Whithorn D & G 40 E7
Whiting Bay N Ayrs 44 E5
Whitland Carmth 18 E5
Whitley Bay N Tyne 43 K5
Whitley Chapel
  Nthumb 43 G6
Whitminster Gloucs 13 H1
Whitstable Kent 11 J2
Whittington Shrops 27 L6
Whittlebury Nhants 23 G6
Whittlesey Cambs 24 A6
Whitton Powys 21 G4
Whitwell Derbys 30 B3
Whitwell Herts 15 J2
Wick Highld 65 J3
Wickford Essex 16 F7
Wickham Hants 8 F5
Wickham Market
  Suffk 17 K2
Wickwar S Glos 13 H3
Widdrington
  Nthumb 43 K3
Widecombe in the
  Moor Devon 6 A4
Widegates Cnwll 3 J5
Widemouth Bay
  Cnwll 4 B6
Widford Herts 16 C5
Widmerpool Notts 30 C6
Widnes Halton 28 C2
Wigan Gt Man 32 E6
Wiggenhall St
  Germans Norfk 24 D4
Wigston Leics 23 G1
Wigton Cumb 42 A6
Wigtown D & G 40 E6
Wilberfoss E R Yk 34 D2
Wilby Nhants 23 J4
Willand Devon 5 J6
Willingham Cambs 24 B8
Wilmcote Warwks 22 C4
Wilmington Devon 6 F2
Wilmslow Ches E 28 F2
Wilsontown S Lans 46 A4
Wilstead Bed 23 L6
Wilton Wilts 13 L7
Wimblington Cambs 24 B6
Wimborne Minster
  Dorset 8 A5
Wincanton Somset 13 H7
Winchcombe Gloucs 22 B7
Winchelsea E Susx 11 G6
Winchester Hants 8 E3
Windermere Cumb 37 G4
Windsor W & M 15 G6
Wing Bucks 14 F2
Wingate Dur 43 L7
Wingham Kent 11 K3
Winkfield Br For 14 F6
Winkleigh Devon 4 F6
Winscombe N Som 12 E5
Winsford Ches W 28 D3
Winsford Somset 5 H4
Winsham Somset 7 G2
Winslow Bucks 23 H7
Winster Derbys 29 J4
Winterborne
  Monkton Dorset 7 J3
Winterborne
  Stickland Dorset 7 L2
Winterborne
  Whitechurch
  Dorset 7 L2
Winterbourne
  Abbas Dorset 7 J3
Winterbourne Stoke
  Wilts 13 L7
Winteringham N Linc 34 F5
Winterslow Wilts 8 C3
Winterton N Linc 34 F5
Winwick Cambs 23 L3
Wirksworth Derbys 29 J4
Wisbech Cambs 31 K8
Wisborough Green
  W Susx 9 K3
Wishaw N Lans 45 L3
Witham Essex 16 F5
Witheridge Devon 5 G6
Withern Lincs 31 K2
Withernsea E R Yk 35 K4
Withington Gloucs 22 B8
Withington Herefs 21 J6
Withyham E Susx 10 D5
Withypool Somset 5 H4
Witnesham Suffk 17 J3
Witney Oxon 14 B3
Wittersham Kent 11 G5
Witton le Wear Dur 43 J8
Wiveliscombe
  Somset 5 J4
Wivelsfield E Susx 10 C6
Wivenhoe Essex 17 H5
Wix Essex 17 J4
Woburn C Beds 23 K6
Woking Surrey 15 G7
Wokingham Wokham 14 F6
Wolf's Castle Pembks 18 C4
Wollaston Nhants 23 J4
Wollaston Shrops 27 L8
Wolsingham Dur 43 H7
Wolverhampton
  Wolves 21 M1
Wolvey Warwks 23 E2
Wolviston S on T 38 E2
Wombourne Staffs 21 M2
Wombwell Barns 34 B6
Wooburn Bucks 14 F5
Woodbridge Suffk 17 K3
Woodchurch Kent 11 G5
Woodford Gloucs 13 G2
Woodhall Spa Lincs 31 H4
Woodland Dur 38 B2
Woodstock Oxon 14 C3
Woofferton Shrops 21 J4
Wookey Hole
  Somset 12 F6
Wool Dorset 7 L3
Woolacombe Devon 4 D3
Wooler Nthumb 47 K6
Woolhampton
  W Berk 14 D6
Woolpit Suffk 17 H2
Woore Shrops 28 E5
Wootton N Linc 35 G6
Wootton Oxon 14 B2
Wootton Bassett
  Wilts 13 L3
Wootton Courtenay
  Somset 5 H4
Wootton Wawen
  Warwks 22 C4
Worcester Worcs 21 M5
Workington Cumb 36 D1
Worksop Notts 30 C2
Worlingworth Suffk 17 K1
Wormit Fife 51 J4
Worplesdon Surrey 15 G7
Worthen Shrops 21 G1
Worthing W Susx 9 L5
Worth Matravers
  Dorset 7 M4
Wotton-under-Edge
  Gloucs 13 H3
Wragby Lincs 31 G3
Wrangaton Devon 6 A6
Wrangle Lincs 31 K5
Wrawby N Linc 35 G6
Wrelton N York 39 G5
Wrentham Suffk 25 L7
Wrestlingworth
  C Beds 16 B3
Wrexham Wrexhm 27 L5
Wroughton Swindn 13 L4
Wroxall IoW 8 F7
Wroxeter Shrops 28 D8
Wroxham Norfk 25 K4
Wroxton Oxon 22 E6
Wyboston Bed 23 L5
Wye Kent 11 H4
Wylye Wilts 13 K7
Wymondham Leics 30 E7
Wymondham Norfk 25 H5

Y

Yarcombe Devon 6 F2
Yardley Gobion
  Nhants 23 H5
Yardley Hastings
  Nhants 23 J5
Yarm S on T 38 D3
Yarmouth IoW 8 D6
Yarrowford Border 46 E6
Yateley Hants 14 F7
Yatton N Som 12 E5
Yatton Keynell Wilts 13 J4
Yaxley Cambs 23 M2
Yeadon Leeds 33 K3
Yealmpton Devon 3 L5
Yelverton Devon 3 L4
Yelverton Norfk 25 K5
Yeovil Somset 7 H1
Yeovilton Somset 12 F8
Yetts o'Muckhart
  Clacks 50 E6
Y Felinheli Gwynd 26 D3
Y Maerdy Conwy 27 J5
York C York 34 C2
Youlgreave Derbys 29 J4
Yoxall Staffs 29 H7
Yoxford Suffk 17 L1
Y Rhiw Gwynd 26 B6
Ysbyty Ystwyth
  Cerdgn 20 B3
Ystalyfera Neath 19 K5
Ystradgynlais Powys 19 K5
Ystrad Mynach
  Caerph 12 C2

Z

Zeals Wilts 13 H7
Zennor Cnwll 2 B6

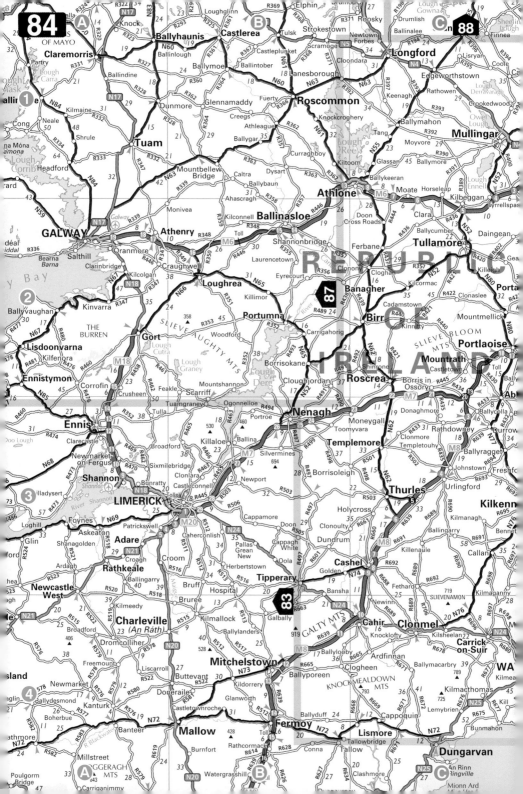

Ceann Iorrais
Erris Head
Cuan an
Inbhir
Mhóir
Downpatrick Head

Béal an Mhuirthead
Belmullet
R314
Ballycastle
75
R314
Killala
Bay
Easky
R297
60
Inishcrone
51
Dro

Inis Gé Thuaidh
Inishkea North
Bun na hAbhna
Bunnahowen
R313
19
Carrowmore
Lake
Bangor
Erris
N59
43
Ballina
N59
Bunnyconnellan
Slieve Gamph or The
31

Inis Gé Theas
Inishkea South
Crossmolina
R315
Killala
N59
Tobe

Dubh Oileán Mór
*Duvillaun
More*
Cuan an
Fhóid Dhuibh
Blacksod Bay
31
719
SLIEVE CARR
R312
N26
Slieve Gamph or The
31

Achill
Head
671
SLIEVEMORE
Keel
R319
27
N59
NEPHIN BEG RANGE
55
806
NEPHIN
R315
13
Foxford
Charleston

Achill Island
Oileán Acla
Mulrany
37
R311
Lough
Feeagh
R317
R312
R310
Swinford
N26

R310
Turlough
24
24
N5
R320
Irelo

Clare Island
Newport
R311
Castlebar
17
N5
Ballyhean
Kiltamagh
29
R321
Kilkelly
R322
N26
Knoc

Clew Bay
Westport
31
N5
29
Balla
R324
14
R323

Inishturk
Caher
Island
Louisburgh
R335
21
R330
29
N84
**PLAINS
OF MAYO**
R320
19

Inishbofin
R378
762
CROAGH PATRICK
32
Partry
Claremorris
R331
Ballindine
N17

Inishshark
31
R335
N59
32
Lough
Mask
Lough
Carra
21

Renvyle
Leenane
673
R330
Ballinrobe
N84
Kilmaine
31
N17
29
R332

Letterfrack
R344
14
R336
An Fhairche
Clonbur
Cong
Neale
50
48
Shrule
R334

R379
34
Clifden
N59
Sraith Salach
Recess
R345
Corr na Móna
Cornamona
R333

Ballyconneely
R341
R342
19
R340
16
7
Lough
Corrib
64
Headford
32

Slyne Head
42
Cashel
R340
R336
Oughterard
N84

Roundstone
Carna
Carna
Glinsce
Glinsk
47
43
N59
Galway

Cruach na Caoile
*Croaghnakeela
Island*
Cill Chiaráin
Kilkieran
N17
N18

Garumna
*Gorumna
Island*
An Spidéal
Spiddal
50
R336
GALWAY
Orann

An Sunda ó Thuaidh
North Sound
Bearna
Barna
Salthill
Clarinbridge
K
N1

Inis Mór
Inishmore
Galway Bay
N67

Oileáin Árann
Aran Islands
Inis Meáin
Inishmaan
Ballyvaughan
30
17
Kinvarra
R347

Inis Óirr
Inisheer
South
Sound
R477
R67
R480
**THE
BURREN**

Doolin
Lisdoonvarna
M18

R478
Kilfenora
R476
R460
16

Liscannor
R478
Ennistymon
Corrofin
23
Crush

Hags Head
Lahinch
N85
45
R476
6

Mal Bay
Milltown Malbay
N67
27
Ennis

Spanish Point
R460
31
11

Doo Lough
Clarecastle
Newmarket-
on-Fergus

82

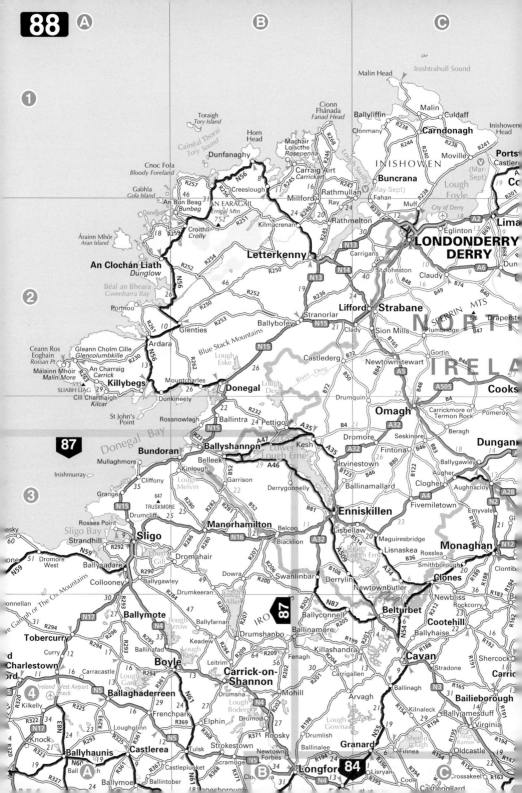

Distance chart - Ireland

This chart shows distances, in both miles and kilometres, between two towns along AA-recommended routes. Using motorways and other main roads this is normally the fastest route, though not necessarily the shortest.

For example, the distance between Cork and Omagh is 435 kilometres or 270 miles (8 kilometres is approximately 5 miles).

Distances in miles

```
99  41 168  83 196 246  84  53  86  33  96  93 167  50 150 299 164 274  62 208  71 233  37 138  68 101  92 197 268 145 186 313 180 123
    148 123  95 101 136 113 144  78  93 150  89  68  84  57 189  76 142 170  74 145 115 111  45 160  20  74  89 138  28 114 182 116 111
        202 117 230 264 116  22 105  51 129 111 251  84 231 319 182 294  22 228  72 252  70 156  63 142 126 215 288 165 205 333 200 143
             98  91 231 116 212 189 195  53 201 144 118 111 274 199 236 223 167 161 210 144 169 199 103  76 191 232 147 236 277 239 216
                153 187  69 100  68  61 106  84 121 132 103 239 143 193 109 125  93 166  59  90 109  55  70 139 189 168 233 161 104
                    170 144 240 177 196 181 187  91 146  50 215 179 178 251 113 189 150 172 148 227  98 104 138 171 125 189 216 218 207
                        248 257 157 213 285 167  87 214 122  57  92  56 286  64 304  22 270 108 308 156 208  64  76 129  80  99 112 185
                            127 143 111  36 156 161  42 128 285 215 248 120 184  46 220  47 159  84  93  40 209 242 138 240 287 229 172
                                 98  44 144 104 246  95 226 314 175 289  44 223  93 245  80 155  85 146 136 214 282 160 198 327 194 138
                                     53 176   8 147  99 129 214  80 192 126 124 151 150 112  54 150  96 133 114 182  66 103 227  92  35
                                        131  59 168  64 152 266 130 241  73 175  99 200  65 105  98 102 105 164 235  81 153 280 147  90
                                            178 198  74 165 322 251 284 136 221  61 256  59 196  91 130  77 246 278 175 253 323 269 212
                                                152 114 139 221  85 197 133 129 153 155 119  59 160 107 139 119 193  71 110 238  83  26
                                                    153  42 130 122  92 273  23 207  66 186  91 229  86 122  47  88 101 101 133 139 174
                                                        136 270 173 225 106 157  61 198  27 122  98  86  41 170 221 100 198 265 192 135
                                                            172 131 134 223  64 173 102 165 101 210  49  88  89 124  80 142 169 171 159
                                                                155  63 306  57 241  97 222 125 263 127 156  82  43 137 135  96 173 208
                                                                    121 200  75 224  80 189  31 228  96  50  51 139  51  30 172  65  87
                                                                        315  70 285  42 251 136 339 162 208  92  20 137 119  50 157 216
                                                                            250  75 273  75 178  55 164 147 241 310 187 226 355 222 165
                                                                                219  43 183  68 273  94 145  25  65  69  78 110 116 151
                                                                                    296  34 202  40 137  85 261 280 161 250 325 242 185
                                                                                        260  95 298 136 181  51  63 116  78  92 116 175
                                                                                            168  71 114  68 227 247 127 215 292 203 147
                                                                                                205  66 120  59 132  21  66 177  70  82
                                                                                                    163 122 278 347 224 267 392 259 202
                                                                                                         53 109 158  44 134 203 136 129
                                                                                                            169 202  98 186 247 190 159
                                                                                                                 88  80  53 133  91 141
                                                                                                                    133 139  53 177 215
                                                                                                                         87 178  91  93
                                                                                                                            170  38  80
                                                                                                                                208 256
                                                                                                                                     59
```

Diagonal labels (left→right): Armagh, Athlone, Belfast, Béal an Mhuirthead Belmullet, Cavan, Clifden, Cork, Donegal, Downpatrick, Dublin, Dundalk, An Clochán Liath Dunglow, Dún Laoghaire, Ennis, Enniskillen, Galway, Kilkee, Kilkenny, Killarney, Larne, Limerick, Londonderry Derry, Mallow, Omagh, Portlaoise, Portrush, Roscommon, Sligo, Tipperary, Tralee, Tullamore, Waterford, An Coireán Waterville, Wexford, Wicklow

```
159
 66 238
270 198 324
144  84 141 238
315 163 370 147 246
396 218 425 371 300 274
135 182 187 187 111 232 399
 85 232  35 342 161 387 414 204
139 125 169 305 109 285 253 230 157
 53 150  83 314  99 316 342 179  71  85
155 242 207 246 171 291 459  58 232 283 211
150 143 179 324 135 301 269 251 167  13  95 287
269 110 404 232 194 146 103 296 396 236 271 319 245
 81 135 135 189  52 235 345  68 152 159 102 119 184 245
241  91 372 179 166  80 196 205 364 208 244 265 224  67 219
324 176 259 287 261 202 188 315 449 291 329 375 300  55 309 123
257 122 287 321 230 288 148 346 282 123 204 404 137 196 279 211 250
441 228 473 380 310 287  90 399 465 309 388 457 317 149 363 216 101 195
100 274  36 359 175 404 460 193  71 203 117 219 214 440 170 359 493 322 507
335 119 367 268 201 184 103 296 359 199 282 356 208  37 252 104  92 121 112 403
114 233 115 259 149 305 490  74 150 242 159  98 246 333  98 278 388 361 481 120 353
376 185 405 338 268 242  35 354 394 241 322 412 250 106 319 164 156 129  67 440  69 477
 60 178 112 232  95 277 435  75 129 180 104  95 192 300  43 266 357 304 405 120 295  55 419
222  73 251 272 145 238 173 256 250  87 168 315  95 146 197 163 202  49 219 286 110 325 153 271
109 258 101 319 175 365 496 135 136 242 158 147 258 369 158 338 424 367 546  89 440  64 480 115 330
163  32 299 166  88 157 251 150 235 155 164 209 172 139 138  78 205 155 261 263 152 221 219 184 106 262
147 118 202 123 112 168 335  64 219 214 169 123 224 196  67 141 252 241 335  63 291 110 192 193  86
317 143 347 308 224 223 102 336 345 183 263 396 192  76 274 144 132  82 148 388  40 420  82 366  95 447 176 272
432 221 464 374 303 275 122 390 454 293 378 448 311 142 355 200  69 223  33 499 105 451  99 398 212 559 254 325 141
233  45 266 237 109 201 207 221 258 106 131 281 113 163 161 129 221  83 221 301 111 259 189 204  34 361  71 158 128 214
301 184 330 380 271 304 129 386 320 167 248 444 177 162 319 229 218  48 192 366 126 403 125 346 106 431 216 300  86 224 140
504 294 536 446 376 348 159 462 527 366 451 520 383 214 427 272 154 277  82 572 177 523 148 470 285 631 327 398 214  85 286 273
290 186 322 385 260 351 180 370 312 148 237 433 134 223 310 275 278 105 253 357 186 390 187 327 113 417 219 305 147 285 147  61 334
198 178 230 348 166 333 298 276 222  56 145 341  42 280 217 256 335 140 348 266 243 298 282 236 131 325 207 256 227 346 150 129 412  95
```

Distances in kilometres

A

Abbeydorney Kerry 82 C2
Abbeyfeale Limrck 82 C2
Abbeyleix Laois 84 C3
Adamstown Wexfd 85 D4
Adare Limrck 83 C2
Adrigole Cork 82 C3
Aghadowey Lderry 89 D2
Ahascragh Galway 87 D3
Ahoghill Antrim 89 D2
Allihies Cork 82 B3
Anascaul Kerry 82 B2
An Bun Beag Donegl 88 B2
An Charraig Donegl 88 A2
An Clochán Liath
    Donegl 88 A2
An Coireán Kerry 82 B3
An Daingean Kerry 82 B2
An Fhairche Galway 86 C3
Annalong Down 89 E4
Annestown Watfd 84 C4
An Rinn Watfd 83 F3
An Spidéal Galway 86 C3
Antrim Antrim 89 D2
Ardagh Limrck 83 D2
Ardara Donegl 88 A2
Ardee Louth 89 D4
Ardfert Kerry 82 C2
Ardfinnan Tippry 84 C4
Ardglass Down 89 E3
Ardgroom Cork 82 B3
Ardmore Watfd 83 E3
Arklow Wicklw 85 E3
Arless Laois 85 D3
Armagh Armagh 89 D3
Armoy Antrim 89 D1
Arthurstown Wexfd 85 D4
Arvagh Cavan 88 B4
Ashbourne Meath 85 E1
Ashford Wicklw 85 E2
Askeaton Limrck 83 D1
Athboy Meath 85 D1
Athea Limrck 82 C2
Athenry Galway 87 D3
Athleague Roscom 87 D3
Athlone Wmeath 84 C1
Athy Kildre 85 D2
Augher Tyrone 88 C3
Aughnacloy Tyrone 88 C3
Aughrim Wicklw 85 E3
Avoca Wicklw 85 E3

B

Bagenalstown Carlow 85 D3
Baile Mhic Íre Cork 82 C3
Bailieborough Cavan 88 C4
Balbriggan Dublin 85 E1
Balla Mayo 86 C2
Ballaghaderreen
    Roscom 87 D2
Ballina Mayo 86 C2
Ballina Tippry 83 D1
Ballinafad Sligo 87 D2
Ballinagh Cavan 88 C4
Ballinakill Laois 84 C3
Ballinalee Longfd 88 B4
Ballinamallard
    Ferman 88 B3
Ballinamore Leitrm 88 B4
Ballinascarty Cork 83 D3

Ballinasloe Galway 87 D3
Ballindine Mayo 86 C3
Ballineen Cork 83 D3
Ballingarry Limrck 83 D2
Ballingarry Tippry 84 C3
Ballingeary Cork 82 C3
Ballinhassig Cork 83 D3
Ballinlough Roscom 87 D2
Ballinrobe Mayo 86 C3
Ballinspittle Cork 83 D3
Ballintober Roscom 87 D2
Ballintra Donegl 88 B3
Ballivor Meath 85 D1
Ballon Carlow 85 D3
Ballybaun Galway 87 D3
Ballybay Monhan 88 C4
Ballybofey Donegl 88 B2
Ballybunion Kerry 82 C2
Ballycanew Wexfd 85 E3
Ballycarry Antrim 89 E2
Ballycastle Antrim 89 D1
Ballycastle Mayo 86 C1
Ballyclare Antrim 89 E2
Ballycolla Laois 84 C3
Ballyconneely Galway 86 B3
Ballyconnell Cavan 88 B4
Ballycotton Cork 83 E3
Ballydehob Cork 82 C4
Ballydesmond Cork 82 C2
Ballyduff Kerry 82 C2
Ballyduff Watfd 84 B4
Ballyfarnan Roscom 87 D2
Ballygalley Antrim 89 E2
Ballygar Galway 87 D3
Ballygawley Sligo 87 D1
Ballygawley Tyrone 88 C3
Ballygowan Down 89 E3
Ballyhack Wexfd 85 D4
Ballyhaise Cavan 88 C4
Ballyhale Dublin 85 D3
Ballyhaunis Mayo 87 D2
Ballyhean Mayo 86 C2
Ballyheige Kerry 82 C2
Ballyjamesduff Cavan 88 C4
Ballykeeran Wmeath 84 C1
Ballylanders Limrck 83 E2
Ballylickey Cork 82 C3
Ballyliffin Donegl 88 C1
Ballylongford Kerry 82 C2
Ballylooby Tippry 84 B4
Ballylynan Laois 85 D2
Ballymacarbry Watfd 84 C4
Ballymahon Longfd 84 C1
Ballymakeery Cork 82 C3
Ballymena Antrim 89 D2
Ballymoe Galway 87 D2
Ballymoney Antrim 89 D2
Ballymore Wmeath 84 C1
Ballymore Eustace
    Kildre 85 D2
Ballymote Sligo 87 D2
Ballynahinch Down 89 E3
Ballynure Antrim 89 E2
Ballyporeen Tippry 84 B4
Ballyragget Kilken 84 C3
Ballyroan Laois 84 C3
Ballyronan Lderry 89 D2
Ballysadare Sligo 87 D1
Ballyshannon Donegl 87 D1
Ballyvaughan Clare 86 C4
Ballywalter Down 89 E3
Balrothery Dublin 85 E1
Baltimore Cork 82 C4
Baltinglass Wicklw 85 D2

Banagher Offaly 84 B2
Banbridge Down 89 D3
Bandon Cork 83 D3
Bangor Down 89 E2
Bangor Erris Mayo 86 B2
Bansha Tippry 84 B3
Banteer Cork 83 D2
Bantry Cork 82 C3
Barna Galway 86 C3
Béal an Mhuirthead
    Mayo 86 B1
Béal Átha an
    Ghaorthaidh Cork 82 C3
Bearna Galway 86 C3
Beaufort Kerry 82 C3
Belcoo Ferman 87 E1
Belfast Belfst 89 E3
Belgooly Cork 83 D3
Bellaghy Lderry 89 D2
Belleek Ferman 87 D1
Belmullet Mayo 86 B1
Belturbet Cavan 88 C4
Benburb Tyrone 89 D3
Bennettsbridge
    Kilken 85 D3
Beragh Tyrone 88 C3
Bettystown Meath 85 E1
Birr Offaly 84 C2
Blacklion Cavan 87 E1
Blackrock Dublin 85 E2
Blackwater Wexfd 85 E3
Blarney Cork 83 D3
Blessington Wicklw 85 D2
Boherbue Cork 83 D2
Borris Carlow 85 D3
Borris in Ossory Laois 84 C2
Borrisokane Tippry 87 D4
Borrisoleigh Tippry 84 C3
Boyle Roscom 87 D2
Bracknagh Offaly 85 D2
Bray Wicklw 85 E2
Bridgetown Wexfd 85 D4
Brittas Dublin 85 E2
Broadford Clare 83 D1
Broadford Limrck 83 D2
Broughshane Antrim 89 D2
Bruff Limrck 83 D2
Bruree Limrck 83 D2
Bunbeg Donegl 88 B2
Bunclody Wexfd 85 D3
Buncrana Donegl 88 C1
Bundoran Donegl 87 D1
Bunmahon Watfd 84 C4
Bun na hAbhna Mayo 86 B1
Bunnahowen Mayo 86 B1
Bunnyconnellan Mayo 86 C2
Bunratty Clare 83 D1
Burnfort Cork 83 D3
Bushmills Antrim 89 D1
Buttevant Cork 83 D2

C

Cadamstown Offaly 84 C2
Caherconlish Limrck 83 D1
Caherdaniel Kerry 82 B3
Cahersiveen Kerry 82 B3
Cahir Tippry 84 C4
Caledon Tyrone 88 C3
Callan Kilken 84 C3
Caltra Galway 87 D3
Camp Kerry 82 B2
Campile Wexfd 85 D4

Cappagh White
    Tippry 84 B3
Cappamore Limrck 83 E1
Cappoquin Watfd 84 C4
Carlanstown Meath 85 D1
Carlingford Louth 89 D4
Carlow Carlow 85 D3
Carna Galway 86 B3
Carndonagh Donegl 88 C1
Carnew Wicklw 85 E3
Carnlough Antrim 89 E2
Carracastle Mayo 87 D2
Carraig Airt Donegl 88 B1
Carrick Donegl 88 A2
Carrickart Donegl 88 B1
Carrickfergus Antrim 89 E2
Carrickmacross
    Monhan 89 D4
Carrickmore or
    Termon Rock
    Tyrone 88 C3
Carrick-on-Shannon
    Leitrm 87 D2
Carrick-on-Suir Tippry 84 C4
Carrigahorig Tippry 87 D4
Carrigaline Cork 83 D3
Carrigallen Leitrm 88 B4
Carriganimmy Cork 83 D3
Carrigans Donegl 88 C2
Carrigtohill Cork 83 E3
Carryduff Down 89 E3
Cashel Galway 86 B3
Cashel Tippry 84 C3
Castlebar Mayo 86 C2
Castlebellingham
    Louth 89 D4
Castleblayney Monhan 89 D4
Castlebridge Wexfd 85 E4
Castlecomer Kilken 85 D3
Castleconnell Limrck 83 D1
Castlederg Tyrone 88 B2
Castledermot Kildre 85 D2
Castlegregory Kerry 82 B2
Castleisland Kerry 82 C2
Castlemaine Kerry 82 C2
Castlemartyr Cork 83 E3
Castleplunket Roscom 87 D2
Castlepollard Wmeath 84 C1
Castlerea Roscom 87 D2
Castlerock Lderry 88 C1
Castleshane Monhan 88 C3
Castletown Laois 84 C2
Castletown
    Bearhaven Cork 82 B3
Castletownroche
    Cork 83 D2
Castletownshend
    Cork 82 C4
Castlewellan Down 89 E3
Cathair Dónall Kerry 82 B3
Causeway Kerry 82 C2
Cavan Cavan 88 C4
Celbridge Kildre 85 D2
Charlestown Mayo 86 C2
Charleville Cork 83 D2
Cheekpoint Watfd 85 D4
Cill Charthaigh Donegl 88 A2
Cill Chiaráin Galway 86 B3
Clady Tyrone 88 C2
Clane Kildre 85 D2
Clara Offaly 84 C2
Clarecastle Clare 83 D1
Claremorris Mayo 86 C2
Clarinbridge Galway 86 C3
Clashmore Watfd 83 E3

Claudy Lderry..................88 C2
Clifden Galway..................86 B3
Cliffony Sligo..................87 D1
Clogh Kilken..................85 D3
Cloghan Offaly..................84 C2
Clogheen Tippry..................84 B4
Clogher Tyrone..................88 C3
Clohamon Wexfd..................85 D3
Clonakilty Cork..................83 D4
Clonard Meath..................85 D1
Clonaslee Laois..................84 C2
Clonbulloge Offaly..................85 D2
Clonbur Galway..................86 C3
Clondalkin Dublin..................85 E2
Clones Monhan..................88 C3
Clonlara Clare..................83 D1
Clonmany Donegl..................88 C1
Clonmel Tippry..................84 C4
Clonmellon Wmeath..................85 D1
Clonmore Tippry..................84 C3
Clonony Offaly..................84 C2
Clonoulty Tippry..................84 C3
Clonroche Wexfd..................85 D3
Clontibret Monhan..................88 C3
Cloondara Longfd..................84 C1
Clough Down..................89 E3
Cloughjordan Tippry..................87 E4
Cloyne Cork..................83 E3
Coagh Tyrone..................89 D2
Coalisland Tyrone..................89 D3
Cobh Cork..................83 E3
Coleraine Lderry..................89 D1
Collinstown Wmeath..................85 D1
Collon Louth..................89 D4
Collooney Sligo..................87 D1
Comber Down..................89 E3
Cong Mayo..................86 C3
Conna Cork..................83 E3
Cookstown Tyrone..................89 D2
Coole Wmeath..................84 C1
Cooraclare Clare..................82 C1
Cootehill Cavan..................88 C4
Cork Cork..................83 D3
Cornamona Galway..................86 C3
Corr na Móna Galway..................86 C3
Corrofin Clare..................86 C4
Courtmacsherry Cork..................83 D3
Courtown Wexfd..................85 E3
Craigavon Armagh..................89 D3
Craughwell Galway..................87 D3
Crawfordsburn Down..................89 E2
Creegs Galway..................87 D3
Creeslough Donegl..................88 B1
Croagh Limrck..................83 D2
Croithlí Donegl..................88 B2
Crolly Donegl..................88 B2
Crookedwood
   Wmeath..................84 C1
Crookhaven Cork..................82 C4
Crookstown Cork..................83 D3
Croom Limrck..................83 D2
Crossakeel Meath..................85 D1
Cross Barry Cork..................83 D3
Crosshaven Cork..................83 E3
Crossmaglen Armagh..................89 D4
Crossmolina Mayo..................86 C2
Crumlin Antrim..................89 D2
Crusheen Clare..................86 C4
Culdaff Donegl..................88 C1
Cullybackey Antrim..................89 D2
Curracloe Wexfd..................85 E4
Curraghboy Roscom..................87 D3
Curry Sligo..................87 D2
Cushendall Antrim..................89 D2
Cushendun Antrim..................89 D1

D

Daingean Offaly..................84 C2
Delgany Wicklw..................85 E2
Delvin Wmeath..................85 D1
Derry Lderry..................88 C2
Derrygonnelly
   Ferman..................87 E1
Derrylin Ferman..................88 B3
Dervock Antrim..................89 D1
Dingle Kerry..................82 B2
Doagh Antrim..................89 D2
Donaghadee Down..................89 E2
Donaghmore Laois..................84 C3
Donard Wicklw..................85 D2
Donegal Donegl..................88 B2
Doneraile Cork..................83 D2
Doolin Clare..................86 C4
Doon Limrck..................83 E1
Doonbeg Clare..................82 C1
Doon Cross Roads
   Offaly..................84 C2
Douglas Cork..................83 D3
Downpatrick Down..................89 E3
Dowra Cavan..................87 E1
Draperstown
   Lderry..................89 D2
Drimoleague Cork..................82 C3
Dripsey Cork..................83 D3
Drogheda Louth..................85 E1
Dromahair Leitrm..................87 D1
Dromcolliher Limrck..................83 D2
Dromore Down..................89 D3
Dromore Tyrone..................88 C3
Dromore West Sligo..................86 C1
Drumcliff Sligo..................87 D1
Drumcondra Meath..................89 D4
Drumkeeran Leitrm..................87 D1
Drumlish Longfd..................88 B4
Drumod Leitrm..................87 E2
Drumquin Tyrone..................88 C3
Drumshanbo Leitrm..................87 E2
Drumsna Leitrm..................87 E2
Duagh Kerry..................82 C2
Dublin Dublin..................85 E2
Duleek Meath..................85 E1
Dunboyne Meath..................85 E1
Duncormick Wexfd..................85 D4
Dundalk Louth..................89 D4
Dunderrow Cork..................83 D3
Dundonald Down..................89 E3
Dundrum Down..................89 E3
Dundrum Tippry..................84 B3
Dunfanaghy Donegl..................88 B1
Dungannon Tyrone..................89 D3
Dungarvan Kilken..................85 D3
Dungarvan Watfd..................83 F3
Dungiven Lderry..................88 C2
Dunglow Donegl..................88 A2
Dungourney Cork..................83 E3
Dunkineely Donegl..................88 A2
Dún Laoghaire
   Dublin..................85 E2
Dunlavin Wicklw..................85 D2
Dunleer Louth..................89 D4
Dunloy Antrim..................89 D2
Dunmanway Cork..................82 C3
Dunmore Galway..................87 D3
Dunmore East Watfd..................85 D4
Dunmurry Antrim..................89 E3
Dunshaughlin Meath..................85 D1
Durrow Laois..................84 C3
Durrus Cork..................82 C4
Dysart Roscom..................87 D3

E

Easky Sligo..................86 C1
Edenderry Offaly..................85 D2
Edgeworthstown
   Longfd..................84 C1
Eglinton Lderry..................88 C2
Elphin Roscom..................87 D2
Emyvale Monhan..................88 C3
Enfield Meath..................85 D1
Ennis Clare..................83 D1
Enniscorthy Wexfd..................85 D3
Enniskean Cork..................83 D3
Enniskillen Ferman..................88 B3
Ennistymon Clare..................86 C4
Eyrecourt Galway..................87 D4

F

Fahan Donegl..................88 C2
Farranfore Kerry..................82 C2
Feakle Clare..................87 D4
Fenagh Leitrm..................87 E2
Ferbane Offaly..................84 C2
Fermoy Cork..................83 E2
Ferns Wexfd..................85 E3
Fethard Tippry..................84 C3
Fethard Wexfd..................85 D4
Finnea Wmeath..................88 C4
Fintona Tyrone..................88 C3
Fivemiletown Tyrone..................88 C3
Fontstown Kildre..................85 D2
Foulkesmill Wexfd..................85 D4
Foxford Mayo..................86 C2
Foynes Limrck..................83 D1
Freemount Cork..................83 D2
Frenchpark Roscom..................87 D2
Freshford Kilken..................84 C3
Fuerty Roscom..................87 D3

G

Galbally Limrck..................83 E2
Galway Galway..................86 C3
Garrison Ferman..................87 D1
Garristown Dublin..................85 E1
Garryvoe Cork..................83 E3
Garvagh Lderry..................89 D2
Geashill Offaly..................84 C2
Gilford Down..................89 D3
Glandore Cork..................82 C4
Glanmire Cork..................83 D3
Glanworth Cork..................83 E2
Glaslough Monhan..................88 C3
Glassan Wmeath..................84 C1
Gleann Cholm Cille
   Donegl..................88 A2
Glenarm Antrim..................89 E2
Glenavy Antrim..................89 D3
Glenbeigh Kerry..................82 B3
Glencolumbkille
   Donegl..................88 A2
Glenealy Wicklw..................85 E2
Glengarriff Cork..................82 C3
Glenmore Kilken..................85 D4
Glennamaddy Galway..................87 D3
Glenties Donegl..................88 A2
Glin Limrck..................82 C2
Glinsce Galway..................86 B3
Glinsk Galway..................86 B3

H

Hacketstown Carlow..................85 D3
Headford Galway..................86 C3
Herbertstown Limrck..................83 D2
Hillsborough Down..................89 D3
Hilltown Down..................89 D3
Holycross Tippry..................84 C3
Holywood Down..................89 E2
Horseleap Wmeath..................84 C1
Hospital Limrck..................83 D2
Howth Dublin..................85 E1

I

Inch Kerry..................82 B2
Inchigeelagh Cork..................82 C3
Inishannon Cork..................83 D3
Inishcrone Sligo..................86 C1
Inistioge Kilken..................85 D3
Irvinestown Ferman..................88 B3

J

Johnstown Kilken..................84 C3

K

Kanturk Cork..................83 D2
Keadew Roscom..................87 D2
Keady Armagh..................89 D3
Keel Mayo..................86 B2
Keenagh Longfd..................84 C1
Kells Antrim..................89 D2
Kells Meath..................85 D1
Kenmare Kerry..................82 C3
Kesh Ferman..................88 B3
Kilbeggan Wmeath..................84 C2
Kilberry Meath..................85 D1
Kilbrittain Cork..................83 D3
Kilcar Donegl..................88 A2
Kilcock Kildre..................85 D1
Kilcolgan Galway..................86 C4
Kilconnell Galway..................87 D3
Kilcoole Wicklw..................85 E2
Kilcormac Offaly..................84 C2
Kilcullen Kildre..................85 D2
Kilcurry Louth..................89 D4
Kildare Kildre..................85 D2
Kildavin Carlow..................85 D3
Kildorrery Cork..................83 D2

Golden Tippry..................84 B3
Goleen Cork..................82 C4
Goresbridge Kilken..................85 D3
Gorey Wexfd..................85 E3
Gort Galway..................86 C4
Gortin Tyrone..................88 C2
Gowran Kilken..................85 D3
Graiguenamanagh
   Kilken..................85 D3
Granard Longfd..................88 C4
Grange Sligo..................87 D1
Greenore Louth..................89 D4
Greyabbey Down..................89 E3
Greystones Wicklw..................85 E2
Gulladuff Lderry..................89 D2

Kilfenora Clare 86 C4
Kilgarvan Kerry 82 C3
Kilkee Clare 82 C1
Kilkeel Down 89 E4
Kilkelly Mayo 86 C2
Kilkenny Kilken 84 C3
Kilkieran Galway 86 B3
Kilkinlea Lower Limrck .. 82 C2
Kill Kildre 85 D2
Kill Watfd 84 C4
Killadysert Clare 83 D1
Killala Mayo 86 C1
Killaloe Clare 83 D1
Killarney Kerry 82 C3
Killashandra Cavan 88 C4
Killeagh Cork 83 E3
Killeigh Offaly 84 C2
Killenaule Tippry 84 C3
Killimer Clare 82 C1
Killimor Galway 87 D4
Killiney Dublin 85 E2
Killinick Wexfd 85 E4
Killorglin Kerry 82 C2
Killough Down 89 E3
Killucan Wmeath 85 D1
Killybegs Donegl 88 A2
Killyleagh Down 89 E3
Kilmacanoge Wicklw 85 E2
Kilmacrenan Donegl 88 B2
Kilmacthomas Watfd 84 C4
Kilmaganny Kilken 84 C3
Kilmaine Mayo 86 C3
Kilmallock Limrck 83 D2
Kilmanagh Kilken 84 C3
Kilmeadan Watfd 84 C4
Kilmeage Kildre 85 D2
Kilmeedy Limrck 83 D2
Kilmichael Cork 83 D3
Kilmore Quay Wexfd 85 D4
Kilmuckridge Wexfd 85 E3
Kilnaleck Cavan 88 C4
Kilrea Lderry 89 D2
Kilrush Clare 82 C1
Kilsheelan Tippry 84 C4
Kiltamagh Mayo 86 C2
Kiltealy Wexfd 85 D3
Kiltegan Wicklw 85 D3
Kiltoom Roscom 87 E3
Kingscourt Cavan 89 D4
Kinlough Leitrm 87 D1
Kinnegad Wmeath 85 D1
Kinnitty Offaly 84 C2
Kinsale Cork 83 D3
Kinvarra Galway 86 C4
Kircubbin Down 89 E3
Knock Mayo 86 C2
Knockcroghery
  Roscom 87 D3
Knocklofty Tippry 84 C4
Knocktopher Kilken 85 D3

L

Lahinch Clare 86 C4
Lanesborough Roscom 84 B1
Laragh Wicklw 85 E2
Larne Antrim 89 E2
Lauragh Kerry 82 C3
Laurencetown Galway 87 D3
Leap Cork 82 C4
Leenane Galway 86 B3
Leighlinbridge Carlow 85 D3
Leitrim Leitrm 87 D2

Leixlip Kildre 85 D2
Lemybrien Watfd 84 C4
Letterfrack Galway 86 B3
Letterkenny Donegl 88 B2
Lifford Donegl 88 C2
Limavady Lderry 88 C2
Limerick Limrck 83 D1
Lisbellaw Ferman 88 C3
Lisburn Antrim 89 D3
Liscannor Clare 86 C4
Liscarroll Cork 83 D2
Lisdoonvarna Clare 86 C4
Lismore Watfd 84 C4
Lisnaskea Ferman 88 C3
Lisryan Longfd 84 C1
Listowel Kerry 82 C2
Loghill Limrck 82 C1
Londonderry Lderry 88 C2
Longford Longfd 84 C1
Loughbrickland Down ... 89 D3
Loughgall Armagh 89 D3
Loughglinn Roscom 87 D2
Loughrea Galway 87 D4
Louisburgh Mayo 86 B2
Lucan Dublin 85 E2
Lurgan Armagh 89 D3
Lusk Dublin 85 E1

M

Machair Loiscthe
  Donegl 88 B1
Macroom Cork 83 D3
Maghera Down 89 E3
Maghera Lderry 89 D2
Magherafelt Lderry 89 D2
Maguiresbridge
  Ferman 88 C3
Malahide Dublin 85 E1
Málainn Mhóir Donegl 88 A2
Malin Donegl 88 C1
Malin More Donegl 88 A2
Mallow Cork 83 D2
Manorhamilton Leitrm... 87 D1
Markethill Armagh 89 D3
Martinstown Antrim 89 D2
Maynooth Kildre 85 D1
Mazetown Antrim 89 D3
Middletown Armagh 88 C3
Midleton Cork 83 E3
Millford Donegl 88 B2
Millstreet Cork 83 D3
Milltown Kerry 82 C2
Milltown Malbay Clare ... 82 C1
Mitchelstown Cork 83 E2
Moate Wmeath 84 C1
Mohill Leitrm 87 E2
Monaghan Monhan 88 C3
Monasterevin Kildre 85 D2
Moneygall Offaly 84 C3
Moneymore Lderry 89 D2
Monivea Galway 87 D3
Mooncoin Kilken 84 C4
Moorfields Antrim 89 D2
Mountbellew Bridge
  Galway 87 D3
Mountcharles Donegl 88 B2
Mountmellick Laois 84 C2
Mountrath Laois 84 C2
Mountshannon Clare 87 D4
Moville Donegl 88 C1
Moy Tyrone 89 D3
Moynalty Meath 88 C4

Moyvore Wmeath 84 C1
Muckross Kerry 82 C3
Muff Donegl 88 C2
Mullaghmore Sligo 87 D1
Mullinavat Kilken 85 D4
Mullingar Wmeath 84 C1
Mulrany Mayo 86 B2
Myshall Carlow 85 D3

N

Naas Kildre 85 D2
Naul Dublin 85 E1
Navan Meath 85 D1
Neale Mayo 86 C3
Nenagh Tippry 83 E1
Newbliss Monhan 88 C3
Newbridge Kildre 85 D2
Newcastle Down 89 E3
Newcastle West Limrck .. 83 D2
Newinn Tippry 84 C4
Newmarket Cork 83 D2
Newmarket-on-
  Fergus Clare 83 D1
Newport Mayo 86 B2
Newport Tippry 83 D1
New Ross Wexfd 85 D4
Newry Down 89 D3
Newtown Laois 85 D3
Newtownabbey
  Antrim 89 E2
Newtownards Down 89 E3
Newtownbutler
  Ferman 88 C3
Newtown Forbes
  Longfd 84 C1
Newtownhamilton
  Armagh 89 D3
Newtown Mount
  Kennedy Wicklw 85 E2
Newtownstewart
  Tyrone 88 C2
Nobber Meath 89 D4

O

Ogonnelloe Clare 83 D1
Oilgate Wexfd 85 D4
Oldcastle Meath 88 C4
Omagh Tyrone 88 C3
Omeath Louth 89 D4
Oola Limrck 83 E2
Oranmore Galway 86 C3
Oughterard Galway 86 C3
Ovens Cork 83 D3

P

Pallas Green New
  Limrck 83 E2
Parknasilla Kerry 82 B3
Partry Mayo 86 C2
Passage East Watfd 85 D4
Passage West Cork 83 E3
Patrickswell Limrck 83 D1
Paulstown Kilken 85 D3
Pettigo Donegl 88 B3
Plumbridge Tyrone 88 C2
Pomeroy Tyrone 88 C3

Portadown Armagh 89 D3
Portaferry Down 89 E3
Portarlington Laois 85 D2
Portavogie Down 89 E3
Portballintrae Antrim 89 D1
Portglenone Antrim 89 D2
Portlaoise Laois 84 C2
Portmarnock Dublin 85 E1
Portnoo Donegl 88 A2
Portraine Dublin 85 E1
Portroe Tippry 83 E1
Portrush Antrim 89 D1
Portstewart Lderry 89 D1
Portumna Galway 87 D4
Poulgorm Bridge Kerry . 82 C3
Poyntz Pass Armagh 89 D3

R

Raharney Wmeath 85 D1
Randalstown Antrim 89 D2
Rasharkin Antrim 89 D2
Rathangan Kildre 85 D2
Rathcoole Dublin 85 E2
Rathcormack Cork 83 E3
Rathdowney Laois 84 C3
Rathdrum Wicklw 85 E2
Rathfriland Down 89 D3
Rathkeale Limrck 83 D2
Rathmelton Donegl 88 B2
Rathmolyon Meath 85 D1
Rathmore Kerry 82 C3
Rathmullan Donegl 88 C1
Rathnew Wicklw 85 E2
Rathowen Wmeath 84 C1
Rathvilly Carlow 85 D3
Ratoath Meath 85 E1
Ray Donegl 88 B2
Recess Galway 86 B3
Renvyle Galway 86 B3
Ringaskiddy Cork 83 E3
Ringville Watfd 83 F3
Rockcorry Monhan 88 C4
Roosky Roscom 87 E2
Rosbercon Wexfd 85 D4
Roscommon Roscom 87 D3
Roscrea Tippry 84 C2
Rosepenna Donegl 88 B1
Ross Carbery Cork 83 D4
Rosses Point Sligo 87 D1
Rosslare Wexfd 85 E4
Rosslare Harbour
  Wexfd 85 E4
Rosslea Ferman 88 C3
Rossnowlagh Donegl 88 B3
Rostrevor Down 89 D4
Roundstone Galway 86 B3
Roundwood Wicklw 85 E2
Rush Dublin 85 E1

S

Saintfield Down 89 E3
St Johnston Donegl 88 C2
Sallins Kildre 85 D2
Salthill Galway 86 C3
Scarriff Clare 87 D4
Scartaglin Kerry 82 C2
Scarva Down 89 D3
Schull Cork 82 C4
Scramoge Roscom 87 D2

Seskinore Tyrone............88 C3
Shanagarry Cork............83 E3
Shanagolden Limrck......83 D1
Shankill Dublin...............85 E2
Shannon Clare................83 D1
Shannonbridge Offaly....87 D3
Shercock Cavan...............88 C4
Shillelagh Wicklw............85 D3
Shinrone Offaly...............84 C2
Shrule Mayo....................86 C3
Silvermines Tippry..........83 E1
Sion Mills Tyrone............88 C2
Sixmilebridge Clare........83 D1
Skerries Dublin...............85 E1
Skibbereen Cork.............82 C4
Slane Meath....................85 D1
Sligo Sligo......................87 D1
Smithborough
    Monhan......................88 C3
Sneem Kerry...................82 B3
Spanish Point Clare........82 C1
Spiddal Galway...............86 C3
Sraith Salach Galway......86 B3
Stewartstown Tyrone....89 D3
Stillorgan Dublin.............85 E2
Stonyford Kilken.............85 D3
Strabane Tyrone.............88 C2
Stradbally Laois..............85 D2
Stradone Cavan..............88 C4
Straffan Kildre................85 D2
Strandhill Sligo...............87 D1
Strangford Down............89 E3
Stranorlar Donegl...........88 B2

Strokestown Roscom.....87 D2
Summerhill Meath..........85 D1
Swanlinbar Cavan...........88 B3
Swatragh Lderry.............89 D2
Swinford Mayo................86 C2
Swords Dublin.................85 E1

T

Taghmon Wexfd..............85 D4
Tagoat Wexfd..................85 E4
Tahilla Kerry...................82 B3
Tallaght Dublin................85 E2
Tallow Watfd...................83 E3
Tallowbridge Watfd.........84 B4
Tandragee Armagh..........89 D3
Tang Wmeath..................84 C1
Tarbert Kerry..................82 C1
Templemore Tippry.........84 C3
Templetouhy Tippry........84 C3
Termonfeckin Louth........89 D4
Thomastown Kilken.........85 D3
Thurles Tippry.................84 C3
Timahoe Laois.................85 D2
Timoleague Cork.............83 D3
Tinahely Wicklw..............85 E3
Tipperary Tippry.............84 B3
Tobercurry Sligo.............87 D2
Tobermore Lderry...........89 D2
Toomyvara Tippry............84 B3
Toormore Cork................82 C4

Tralee Kerry....................82 C2
Tramore Watfd................85 D4
Trim Meath......................85 D1
Tuam Galway...................86 C3
Tuamgraney Clare...........83 D1
Tulla Clare......................83 D1
Tullamore Offaly.............84 C2
Tullow Carlow.................85 D3
Tulsk Roscom..................87 D2
Turlough Mayo................86 C2
Tyrrellspass Wmeath......84 C1

U

Urlingford Kilken............84 C3

V

Virginia Cavan.................88 C4

W

Warrenpoint Down..........89 D4
Waterford Watfd.............85 D4
Watergrasshill Cork........83 E3
Waterville Kerry..............82 B3
Westport Mayo................86 C2

Wexford Wexfd...............85 E4
Whitegate Cork...............83 E3
Whitehead Antrim...........89 E2
Wicklow Wicklw...............85 E2
Woodenbridge Wicklw....85 E3
Woodford Galway............87 D4

Y

Youghal Cork...................83 E3